25 Best

MONTRÉAL

How to Use This Book

KEY TO SYMBOLS

✚ Map reference to the accompanying fold-out map

✉ Address

☎ Telephone number

🕙 Opening/closing times

🍴 Restaurant or café

🚆 Nearest rail station

Ⓜ Nearest subway (Metro) station

🚌 Nearest bus route

📷 Nearest riverboat or ferry stop

♿ Facilities for visitors with disabilities

❓ Other practical information

▷ Further information

ℹ Tourist information

✋ Admission charges:
Very expensive (over $50),
Expensive ($25–$50),
Moderate ($10–$50) and
Inexpensive ($10 or less)

This guide is divided into four sections

● Essential Montréal: An introduction to the city and tips on making the most of your stay.

● Montréal by Area: We've broken the city into five areas, and recommended the best sights, shops, entertainment venues, nightlife and restaurants in each one. Suggested walks help you to explore on foot.

● Where to Stay: The best hotels, whether you're looking for luxury, budget or something in between.

● Need to Know: The info you need to make your trip run smoothly, including getting about by public transportation, weather tips, emergency phone numbers and useful websites.

Navigation In the Montréal by Area chapter, we've given each area its own color, which is also used on the locator maps throughout the book and the map on the inside front cover.

Maps The fold-out map with this book is a comprehensive street plan of Montréal. The grid on this fold-out map is the same as the grid on the locator maps within the book. We've given grid references within the book for each sight and listing.

Contents

Introducing Montréal

Montréal is one of the world's great cities, a stylish and laid-back metropolis with superb museums, excellent restaurants, first-rate shopping, a vibrant cultural life and a cosmopolitan population that works and plays with a broad smile on its face.

Nestled between the banks of the Saint Lawrence River and the slopes of Mont-Royal, the heart of the island city is a wonderful mixture of old and new—from the cobbled streets, historic squares and fine buildings of Vieux-Montréal, the city's earliest incarnation after the arrival of French settlers in 1642, to the busy modern streets of downtown, with its many skyscrapers and underground malls and walkways. Farther afield is the site of the 1976 Olympic Games, now an attraction in its own right.

Montréal, of course, owes much of its considerable charm—not least its superb food—to its French heritage, one that has made it the largest French-speaking city in the West after Paris. But to focus only on the city's French élan would be to miss the dynamic influence of its English-speaking residents, a thriving immigrant population of 488,000, and the joie de vivre of a city that is young at heart.

True, there are problems—the winters can be cruel, roadworks never-ending, and Québec's divisive politics maddening—but the old concerns of language, and of Montréal and the rest of Québec splitting from Canada, have now mellowed somewhat. And Montréal is not just about style over substance. The fur trade and river traffic that made it rich may have declined, but this is still a place with a little grit to go with its wit.

So, a piece of Europe in North America? Up to a point. French in taste? Definitely. English? In places, certainly. Canadian? That too. But also a dynamic, fun and fascinating city in its own right—whatever your language and whatever your fancy.

FACTS AND FIGURES

- Population: 1,704,694 (2016 census)
- Percentage of population that is French-speaking: 66 percent
- Ranking: Canada's second-largest city after Toronto
- Area of city: 483sq km (188sq miles)
- Islands making up city: 75
- Height of Mount Royal: 233 metres (764 feet)

PRINTED PAGE

Mordecai Richler brings the vibrant, hard-scrabble life of Montréal's Jewish community to life in the classic *St. Urban's Horseman* and *The Apprenticeship of Duddy Kravitz* (made into a film starring Richard Dreyfuss). Heather O'Neill lovingly depicts Montréal's gritty underbelly in *Lullabies for Little Criminals* and *The Girl Who Was Saturday Night*.

BALCONVILLE

Many Montréalers live in duplexes and triplexes, stacked residences built in the 1930s and 1940s to house the city's blue-collar workers. Curving, wrought-iron staircases link the balconies of the various levels, a building strategy that saved interior space and inadvertently created pleasing places to gather round in the summer.

FAMOUS MONTRÉALERS

Montréal's famous include Prime Minister Justin Trudeau, *Star Trek's* William Shatner, jazz great Oscar Peterson, novelist Mordecai Richler and poet-singer Leonard Cohen. Confederate president Jefferson Davis lived here. Singer Céline Dion was born in Repentigny and film director Denys Arcand was born in Deschambeault.

A Short Stay in Montréal

DAY 1

Morning Begin your day in **place Jacques-Cartier** (▷ 37) in Vieux-Montréal. Walk southwest on rue Notre-Dame Ouest and visit the **Basilique Notre-Dame** (▷ 24–25). Spend the rest of the morning learning about the history of the city at **Pointe-à-Callière** (▷ 30) and its **Musée d'Archéologie et d'Histoire de Montréal**.

Lunch Have a snack at **Olive et Gourmando** (▷ 44), a light meal at Le Petit Dep on St-Paul (▷ 44) or in the **Musée d'Archéologie**, or sample one of the many casual restaurants in the **Vieux-Port** area (▷ 32).

Afternoon If the weather is good, take a boat trip from one of the quays a few moments from the Musée d'Archéologie. Most last 60–90 minutes. If you are traveling with children you may want to visit the **Centre des Sciences de Montréal** (▷ 33–34) and other attractions on the waterfront piers. Then explore **rue Saint-Paul** (▷ 31) and the adjacent streets and squares, especially the **Chapelle Notre-Dame-de-Bon-Secours** (▷ 26) and **Château Ramezay** (▷ 34). The café in the latter makes a delightful place for afternoon tea. Also make time for shopping in the Marché Bonsecours (▷ 27).

Dinner Try **Toque!** (▷ 44), one of Montréal's best restaurants for contemporary cuisine, but book well in advance. For fashionable, meat-free dining, try seriously gorgeous, and seriously delicious, veggie restaurant **LOV** (▷ 44).

Evening Take in a performance at the **Centaur Theatre** (▷ 42) or enjoy a drink with a waterfront view at **Pub St-Paul** (▷ 42). For panoramic rooftop views of Old Montréal, try the 6th floor of l'Auberge du Vieux-Port or the Terrasse Nelligan in the hotel of the same name (▷ 112).

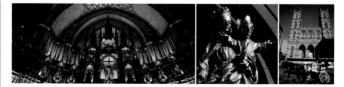

DAY 2

Morning Take a cab close to the Observatoire de l'Est in the **Parc du Mont-Royal** (▷ 72–73) for an overview of the city and a taste of the main park. Walk through the park to Avenue des Pins and then visit the **Musée McCord d'Histoire Canadienne** (▷ 55) and **Musée des Beaux-Arts** (▷ 54) or explore shops and malls such as La Baie d'Hudson (▷ 62) and Centre Eaton (▷ 62) above and below ground near rue Sainte-Catherine.

Lunch Downtown has many sandwich bars and inexpensive restaurants aimed at the area's working population. Or join the in-the-know locals for fresh Moroccan dishes at **Tangia** on Drummond (▷ 66).

Afternoon Either devote the afternoon to the many sights and shops of downtown or take the green Métro line to Pie-IX or Viau to see the sights on and around the **Parc Olympique** (▷ 90–91), especially the **Biodôme** (▷ 86–87) and **Jardin Botanique** (▷ 88–89).

Dinner You have innumerable choices for dinner, including options in the vibrant Quartier Latin, one of the city's main areas for eating, drinking and nightlife. More sedate is boulevard Saint-Laurent above rue Sherbrooke, where you could try **Moishe's** (▷ 81–82), which has been serving sublime steaks since 1938, or **Schwartz's** (▷ 82) for their famous smoked meat.

Evening Head to the **Quartier Latin** (▷ 76) to enjoy its boisterous nightlife or, when in season, attend a ballet or a concert by Montréal's Orchestre Métropolitain. Also, during the summer, there will always be a festival of some sort taking place somewhere in the city. A good place to check is the Quartier des spectacles, next to place des Arts.

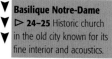

Top 25

TOP 25

ESSENTIAL MONTRÉAL TOP 25

Basilique Notre-Dame
▷ 24–25 Historic church in the old city known for its fine interior and acoustics.

Biodôme de Montréal
▷ 86–87 Four natural habitats representing North and South America.

Canal de Lachine and Marché Atwater ▷ 98 A recreation area and popular market building.

Cathédrale Marie-Reine-du-Monde ▷ 48 A small replica of St. Peter's Basilica in Rome.

Centre Canadien d'Architecture ▷ 49 One of the world's leading architectural museums.

Chapelle Notre-Dame-de-Bon-Secours ▷ 26 Small mariners' chapel dedicated to Ste. Marguerite Bourgeoys.

Christ Church Cathedral ▷ 50 Serene cathedral above an underground shopping mall.

Jardin Botanique de Montréal ▷ 88–89 Spectacular and varied gardens and galleries.

Marché Bonsecours ▷ 27 Graceful landmark building now housing shops and stalls.

McGill University ▷ 52–53 Notable buildings and extensive grounds.

Musée d'Art Contemporain ▷ 51 Works of art from 1939 to the present day.

Musée des Beaux-Arts ▷ 54 Canadian paintings and old masters plus ceramics and furniture.

Musée McCord d'Histoire Canadienne ▷ 55 Excellent native Canadian displays.

Oratoire Saint-Joseph ▷ 70–71 Landmark shrine to St. Joseph built in 1924 with public donations and offering good views.

Parc Jean-Drapeau ▷ 102–103 The park encompasses two islands and includes La Biosphère.

Parc du Mont-Royal ▷ 72–73 Large and attractive park within the city suburbs.

Parc Olympique ▷ 90–91 The striking inclined tower is a major attraction.

Petite Italie ▷ 100–101 Visit for the restaurants and shopping.

Place d'Youville ▷ 28 Evocative market square with a museum presenting the history of the city.

Plateau and Mile End ▷ 74 Popular residential and shopping areas.

Pointe-à-Callière ▷ 30 Archaeological and historical museum in the heart of the old city.

Rue Saint-Paul ▷ 31 See how the city looked in the 19th century.

Saint Patrick's Basilica ▷ 56 Beautiful church often overlooked by visitors.

Underground City ▷ 57 A self-contained city in a warren of underground tunnels.

Vieux-Port ▷ 32 Parks, promenade and boat trips in and from the redeveloped old port.

These pages are a quick guide to the Top 25, which are described in more detail later. Here they are listed alphabetically and the tinted background shows the area they are in.

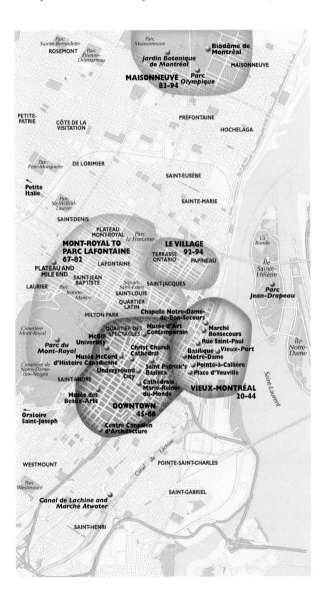

Parc Sainte-Bernadette
ROSEMONT
Parc Étienne-Desmarteau
Parc Maisonneuve
Biodôme de Montréal
Jardin Botanique de Montréal
MAISONNEUVE
MAISONNEUVE 83-94
Parc Olympique

PETITE-PATRIE
CÔTE DE LA VISITATION
PRÉFONTAINE
HOCHELAGA

Parc Père-Marquette
DE LORIMIER
SAINT-EUSÈBE

Petite Italie
Parc Sir-Wilfrid-Laurier
SAINTE-MARIE

SAINT-DENIS

PLATEAU MONT-ROYAL
Parc la Fontaine
MONT-ROYAL TO PARC LAFONTAINE 67-82
LE VILLAGE 92-94
La Ronde
PLATEAU AND MILE END
LAFONTAINE
TERRASSE ONTARIO
PAPINEAU
Île Sainte-Hélène
LAURIER
SAINT-JEAN BAPTISTE
Parc Jeanne-Mance
Square Saint-Louis
SAINT-JACQUES
Parc Jean-Drapeau
SAINT-LOUIS
QUARTIER LATIN
MILTON PARK
Chapelle Notre-Dame-de-Bon-Secours
Marché Bonsecours
Cimetière Mont-Royal
QUARTIER DES SPECTACLES
Musée d'Art Contemporain
Rue Saint-Paul
Île Notre-Dame
Parc du Mont-Royal
McGill University
Christ Church Cathedral
Basilique Notre-Dame
Vieux-Port
Musée McCord d'Histoire Canadienne
Saint Patrick's Basilica
Pointe-à-Callière
Cimetière de Notre-Dame-des-Neiges
Underground City
Place d'Youville
SAINT-ANDRÉ
Cathédrale Marie-Reine-du-Monde
VIEUX-MONTRÉAL 20-44
Musée des Beaux-Arts
DOWNTOWN 45-66
Saint-Laurent
Oratoire Saint-Joseph
Centre Canadien d'Architecture

WESTMOUNT
POINTE-SAINT-CHARLES
Canal de Lachine

Parc Westmount
Canal de Lachine and Marché Atwater
SAINT-GABRIEL

SAINT-HENRI

Shopping

Le shopping—now there's a word that crosses linguistic boundaries. Some Québécois may still *magasinent* (shop) but the truly stylish *font le shopping*.

A Passion for Fashion
Montréal is nothing if not stylish. Indeed, Montréal is Canada's fashion capital, with a clothing industry that is the third-largest in North America. Several fashion schools churn out talent to keep the momentum brisk. And if you're looking for children's clothes, this is the place. Shoppers can find all the best stuff in the city's boutiques and department stores, but serious bargain-hunters head for the northern end of boulevard Saint-Laurent, to the dozens of clothing factories in the Chabanel area that sell to the public on Saturday mornings.

Outdoor Clothing
Trade in animal skins made the city wealthy in the first place, and given the climate, it's not surprising that furs are still popular winter wear. However, some designers have taken a different approach to cold-weather wear. The multilayer winter wear of Kanuk (▷ 78) is stylish and comfortable.

Antiques
Montréal's age makes it a tempting prospect for antiques collectors. Dozens of shops in Westmount, along the west end of rue Notre-Dame between avenue Atwater and rue

SMART SHOPPING

Don't even step into a store here without the ebook of *Smart Shopping Montréal* on your smartphone. Updated every year, this no-nonsense compendium is the guide to everything from haute couture to second-hand furs. Although the emphasis is on where to get the best buys (often at astonishingly low prices), the author has a keen eye for quality. Whether it's children's toys or the best Montréal bagels, this ebook will lead you to it. Download it before you arrive via smartshoppingmontreal.com.

Clockwise from top left: Antiques shops abound; Le Centre Eaton; mouth-watering pastries in a

Guy, as well as in Le Village, cater to just about every taste, with furniture from colonial Québec to 1950s retro. Keep an eye out for rare books, as well as Victorian paintings, religious articles and decorations, china and silverware.

Arts and Crafts
Québec's artistic traditions reach back to the days of New France, when the colony's Catholic bishops kept dozens of artists hard at work, decorating churches with mosaics, paintings, sculptures and stained glass. Dozens of galleries cater to more modern tastes, with work by leading local artists like Paul Fenniak, Betty Goodwin and Jean-Louis Émond. If your tastes lean more to the traditional, consider a startlingly realistic wood carving by a Québec folk artist or a graceful soapstone sculpture by one of Canada's Inuit carvers.

Malls
While trendy shopping areas such as rue Saint-Denis, rue Ste-Catherine in downtown, boulevard Saint-Laurent and, increasingly, Old Montréal take the retail plaudits, don't overlook the joys of shopping under one roof. Montréal makes a great place for pre-Christmas shopping, thanks to its Underground City, which provides protection from the elements. Malls include Cours Mont-Royal, Les Promenades Cathédrale, Le Centre Eaton, place Ville-Marie and place Montréal Trust, all interconnected, near the intersection of rues McGill and Ste-Catherine.

bakery; maple syrup is an ideal souvenir; bustling street markets sell fresh fruit and vegetables

MUSEUM STORES
When you are searching for souvenirs and gifts, don't overlook the stores within museums and art galleries, which generally stock high quality, authentic arts, crafts and design, wonderful books and posters, and sometimes clothing. Particularly good ones include the Musée des Beaux-Arts (▷ 54), the Musée d'Art Contemporain (▷ 51), Pointe-à-Callière (▷ 30, 41) and Musée McCord d'Histoire Canadienne (▷ 55).

Shopping by Theme

Whether you're looking for a department store, a quirky boutique, or something in between, you'll find it all in Montréal. On this page shops are listed by theme. For a more detailed write-up, see the individual listings in Montréal by Area.

Montréal by Night

Montréalers never hibernate, no matter how cold it gets. Saturday-night crowds are almost as large in January as they are in July.

Hot Spots

Downtown, the scene centres on four streets that run between boulevard René-Lévesque and rue Sherbrooke—de la Montagne, Crescent, Bishop and Mackay. They're lined with fine old residences now converted into pubs which appeal to a largely English-speaking crowd. Just as vibrant but more French in ambience is the district around the twin corridors of boulevard Saint-Laurent and rue Saint-Denis. Start around rue Sainte-Catherine and walk away from the river through the Quartier Latin and Plateau Mont-Royal, exploring the cafés and clubs on Rachel. Petite Italie is also buzzing after dark. There's plenty of entertainment in Montréal for all ages and you'll find both languages spoken almost everywhere.

Evening Stroll

Vieux-Montréal has only a few nightclubs, but it's a wonderful place for an evening stroll. Many of the old classical buildings, including the Hôtel de Ville, Place Royale and Château Ramezay, are beautifully illuminated, and a small section of rue Sainte-Hélène is evocatively lit by gas lamps. For an unbeatable view from the river, and a little live music, take a Bateau Mouche dinner cruise (▷ 42).

Party all night at a club, try your luck in a casino, go to rue Ste-Catherine, visit the ballet, or take in some jazz

LONG HISTORY

Montréal has been a popular hot spot with Americans since at least the 1920s and 1930s. During Prohibition, trainloads of fun-seekers from New York and Boston would pour into the city every weekend looking for some excitement and a little legal booze. The city was also popular with African-American jazz musicians, who liked the fact they could pretty much stay and eat wherever they wanted—and date locals without raising so much as an eyebrow.

Where to Eat

Montréal is one of North America's gastronomic capitals, a city that is passionate about its food, and that draws on French and other ethnic culinary influences to offer a wonderfully rich assortment of restaurants, cafés and cuisines.

French Tastes
France is the obvious point of culinary reference, and French-influenced food is the city's most widespread, found not only in restaurants that wouldn't be out of place in Paris, but also in a plethora of cafés and bistros in settings every bit as Gallic as their European counterparts.

Plenty of Choice
The city's rich and multicultural population provides the inspiration for countless other cuisines—from Thai, Vietnamese and Korean to Indian, Chinese and Italian. Not forgetting the classic staples of North America, with some excellent steak houses, plenty of places for pasta, chicken and seafood, and delis for bagels and cured meats.

Where to Go
The key dining areas are well defined, the most popular being rue Saint-Denis and boulevard Saint-Laurent beyond rue Sherbrooke. Here, as in Vieux-Montréal, you are spoiled for choice, though the downtown area, too, has plenty to offer. Also, explore Le Village, the Plateau, Mile End, western rue Notre-Dame and Petite Italie.

PRACTICALITIES

At lunch, look out for set-price two- or three-course menus known as the *spécial du midi*, or midday special. These are good value, as are the two- to four-course set *table d'hôte* menus in the evening. These menus will usually be better value than eating *à la carte*. A multi-course *menu dégustacion*, or tasting menu, will be expensive, but will offer a selection of dishes in small portions, often accompanied by different wines. A starter, or appetizer, in Montréal is called an *entrée*, and the main course is the *plat principal*.

In a city very much influenced by the French, expect to find many atmospheric street cafés and bistros

Where to Eat by Cuisine

There are plenty of places to eat to suit all tastes and budgets in Montréal. On this page they are listed by cuisine. For a more detailed description of each venue, see Montréal by Area.

Breakfast and Brunch
Beauty's (▷ 81)
Première Moisson
   (▷ 106)
Quoi de n'Oeufs (▷ 106)

Cafés and Pâtisseries
Café Bistro (▷ 65)
Olive et Gourmando
   (▷ 44)
Pasticceria Alati-Caserta
   (▷ 106)
Le Petit Dep (▷ 44)
Presse Café (▷ 66)

French and Quebécois Cuisine
Auberge le Saint-Gabriel
   (▷ 43)
Beaver Hall (▷ 65)
Bistrot La Fabrique
   (▷ 81)
Bonaparte (▷ 43)
Boris Bistro (▷ 43)
Chez L'Épicier (▷ 43)
Club Chasse et Peche
   (▷ 43)
L'Express (▷ 81)
The Hambar (▷ 44)
Le Mousso (▷ 94)
Toque! (▷ 44)

Mediterranean
Da Emma (▷ 43)
Graziella (▷ 44)
Moleskine (▷ 82)
L'Omnivore (▷ 82)
Pizzeria Geppetto (▷ 106)
Pizzeria Napoletana
   (▷ 106)
Pizzeria No.900 (▷ 66)
Pullman (▷ 82)

Pan-Asian Cuisine
Bon Blé Riz (▷ 81)
La Maison V.I.P. (▷ 66)
Orchidée de Chine
   (▷ 66)
Ruby Rouge (▷ 66)
Tatami (▷ 44)

Steak and Other Meat
Au Pied de Cochon
   (▷ 81)
L'Entrecôte Saint-Jean
   (▷ 65)
Joe Beef (▷ 106)
Liverpool House (▷ 106)
Moishe's (▷ 81)
Mr. Steer (▷ 66)
Schwartz's (▷ 82)
Uniburger (▷ 82)

Vegetarian
Café Santropol (▷ 81)
Invitation V (▷ 44)
LOV (▷ 44, 65)
Vegano (▷ 82)

World Cuisine
Agrikol (▷ 94)
Brutopia (▷ 65)
Café Ferreira (▷ 65)
Café Sfouf (▷ 94)
Café Stash (▷ 43)
Escondite Cerveceria
   (▷ 65)
Le Taj (▷ 66)
Tangia (▷ 66)

Top Tips For…

However you'd like to spend your time in Montréal, these top suggestions should help you tailor your ideal visit. Each suggestion has a fuller write-up elsewhere in the book.

BURNING THE MIDNIGHT OIL
Board a night-time cruise with disco on the Saint Lawrence river (▷ 33, 42).
Visit the clubs of the Quartier Latin (▷ 80).
Join the revelers in one of downtown's Irish bars, including Pub Le Vieux Dublin (▷ 64).

THE LAP OF LUXURY
Stay on the "Gold Floor" of the Fairmont Le Reine Elizabeth hotel (▷ 112).
Shop 'til you drop at Maison Ogilvy (▷ 63), a luxury department store that has merged with Holt Renfrew, Montréal's other luxury department store.
Go mad among the designer labels showcased in the designer shops on avenue Laurier at the north end of Parc du Mont-Royal (▷ 72–73).

TO KEEP YOUR CHILDREN HAPPY
Stargaze from comfy seats at Rio Tinto Alcan Planetarium (▷ 93).
Go to a performance at TOHU (▷ 105).
Strap them in for a jet-boat trip over the Lachine Rapids (▷ 33).
Hunt for historical treasures in the Labyrinthe du Hangar 16 (▷ 35).
Visit the Insectarium and Biodôme (▷ 86) at the Parc Olympique (▷ 91).

SAVING MONEY
Go to the visitor center in rue Peel (▷ 119) for details of free concerts in churches, parks, malls and the Vieux-Port.
Remember that some museums in Montréal have half-price or reduced entry on certain days and nights, often Wednesday evenings.
Summer festivals such as *Juste Pour Rire* (Just for Laughs) and the International Jazz Festival have many free events (▷ 114).

Clockwise from top left: Downtown gets lively after dark; Montréal International Jazz

TAKING IN THE CULTURE

Attend an ice-hockey game involving Les Canadiens (▷ 64, Centre Bell).

The place des Arts hosts orchestras and leading ballet and opera companies (▷ 64).

Listen to jazz while sipping an artisan brew in a traditional setting at Le Cheval Blanc (▷ 80).

Marvel at the acoustics during an organ recital at the Basilica of Notre-Dame (▷ 24).

For heavenly music, hear the Petits Chanteurs at Oratoire Saint-Joseph (▷ 70) on weekends.

A MEMORABLE PLACE TO STAY

For modern chic, St. Paul Hotel and W Montréal win hands down (▷ 112).

The Hôtel Nelligan is divinely romantic (▷ 112).

Channel your inner student at the surprisingly stylish McGill University (▷ 109).

Calming, historical and well situated on the Golden Mile, Hotel Ambrose is a quirky gem (▷ 109).

Splash out on a penthouse suite at opulent yet contemporary Le Mount Stephen (▷ 112).

ROMANTIC SUPPERS

The Quartier Latin has numerous romantic little bistros (▷ 81–82).

In summer, Boris Bistro's lovely terrace is the place to eat (▷ 43).

For a quirky date, try Agrikol (▷ 94), which has a warm Haitian vibe to melt any heart.

Eat ethically in serene surroundings at vegan restaurant LOV (▷ 44, 65).

A TASTE OF TRADITION

Steaks at Moishe's have been aged and prepared the same way since 1938 (▷ 81).

Classic smoked and cured meats are the specialty of old-world Schwartz's (▷ 82).

Grab a late-night snack at one of Montréal's famous bagel bakeries. They never close.

Indulge in a box of *poutine*, Montréal's inimitable combination of fries, cheese curds and thick gravy (▷ 44). It's tastier than it sounds.

Festival; Nelligan Hotel; stop for a bagel; a stylish room at St. Paul Hotel; powerboat rafting

A BREATH OF FRESH AIR

Clamber to the heights of the Montréal Cross in the Parc du Mont-Royal (▷ 72) and be rewarded with a magnificent view.

Take a turn around the pretty and engaging Jardin Botanique (▷ 88), adjoining Parc Maisonneuve (▷ 93).

Enjoy a brisk stroll or scenic cycle along the Lachine Canal (▷ 98).

Commune with nature at the Pointe-aux-Prairies Nature Park (▷ 105).

SHOPPING UNDER ONE ROOF

La Baie d'Hudson (▷ 62) and **Ogilvy** (▷ 63) are landmark downtown department stores if you're looking for fashion and homeware.

Les Promenades Cathédrale (▷ 63) is a five-layer mall of assorted shops and eating places, beneath Christ Church Cathedral.

The Underground City is a labyrinth of shops sheltered from the elements (▷ 57).

SPECIALTY SHOPPING

Marché Bonsecours (▷ 27) and nearby rue Saint-Paul (▷ 31) are excellent for traditional art, craft and design.

Explore rue St-Denis, south of rue Ste-Catherine, for cutting-edge clothes and trendy stores (▷ 76).

Rue Amherst near rue Ontario and rue Notre-Dame Ouest near rue Guy are great for antiques and retro decor (▷ 78).

CUTTING-EDGE CULTURE

Fine arts and a fine setting define the Musée des Beaux-Arts, Canada's oldest art museum (▷ 54).

Be shocked or amused but never bored at the Musée d'Art Contemporain (▷ 51)—and don't forget to explore its sculpture garden.

Pointe-à-Callière offers Montréal's best interactive history museum (▷ 30).

Engage your eyes, ears and mind with the best contemporary Canadian art at the UQAM Gallery (▷ 75).

From top: the Montréal sky-line; shopping is linked by the Underground City; the Musée des Beaux-Arts

Montréal by Area

Vieux-Montréal

Vieux-Montréal was once the heart of the old city, set around the port, and it still buzzes with life today.

Tour de
l'Horloge

Saint-Laurent

Quai de l'Horloge

**Saint-Laurent
Boat Trips**

*rasses
nsecours*

*Pointe
du Harvre*

Parc
de
Dieppe

Pont de la Concorde

P

**Habitat
'67**

Avenue Pierre- Dupuy

Bassin Bickerdyke

Quai
Mark Drouin

| 0 | | 250 m |
| 0 | | 250 yds |

H   **J**

Basilique Notre-Dame

HIGHLIGHTS

- Pulpit
- Wood carving
- Stained glass
- High altar

No other site in Montréal sums up the city's religious heritage as beautifully as the Basilica of Notre-Dame, where the seductive interior—Romanesque with touches of rococo—lifts you into a world of almost perfect calm.

TIPS

- No more than an hour is needed for a visit.
- Aura, a sound-and-light show by Moment Factory, takes place four to five times a week in the evenings. The cost is $24.50 and tickets can be purchased at aura.ticketpro.ca.

History Founded in 1657, Notre-Dame is located on the flanks of Place d'Armes, the historic focus of the old city. The original church was replaced by the present neo-Gothic basilica between 1824 and 1829. Today the church's twin towers—nicknamed Temperance and Perseverance—still command the skyline. The western tower, built in 1843, contains the famous "Gros Bourdon" ("Large Bumblebee") bell. The bell's rumbling peal can be heard up to 25km (15 miles) away.

Highly decorated Inside, thousands of tiny 24-carat gold stars stud the dusky blue, vaulted ceiling, and 14 stained-glass windows, brought from Limoges in 1929, tell the story of Ville-Marie's early development. But most of the interior is a tribute to the woodworking skills of Québec artists and artisans. All the figures in the life-size tableaus behind the main altar are carved in wood, as is the spectacular pulpit with its curving staircase on the east side of the nave. A fire in 1978 destroyed much of the large chapel behind the main altar. The Sulpician priests who run the church saved what they could of the woodwork and erected an enormous bronze sculpture behind the altar. Now, it serves as a fitting backdrop for the regular organ recitals and concerts that make the most of the basilica's excellent acoustics.

THE BASICS

basiliquenddm.org

🔢 F11

✉️ 110 rue Notre-Dame Ouest

☎️ Basilica 514/842-2925

🕐 Mon–Fri 8–4.30, Sat 8–4, Sun 12.30–4

🚇 Place d'Armes

🚌 38, 55, 129

♿ Very good

💲 Inexpensive

❓ 20-min guided tours in French or English daily included in ticket price. Sound and light show Tue–Sat

Chapelle Notre-Dame-de-Bon-Secours

Glorious statues adorn the Chapelle Notre-Dame-de-Bon-Secours, inside and out

THE BASICS

marguerite-bourgeoys.com

✚ G10

✉ 400 rue Saint-Paul Est

☎ 514/282-8670

🕐 May to mid-Oct Tue–Sun 10–6; mid-Oct to mid-Jan, Mar–Apr Tue–Sun 11–4

🚇 Champ-de-Mars

🚌 14, 129

♿ Poor: four steps to church; no access to tower or museum

👝 Chapel free. Museum moderate

❓ Guided tours of crypt archaeological site (includes museum entry)

HIGHLIGHTS

● Gold Madonna
● Murals
● Votive boats
● Mosaic inlays
● Madonna de Bon-Secours
● "Aerial" chapel
● Views

This tiny building is a monument to Marguerite Bourgeoys, a pious woman dedicated to bringing Christian beliefs to New France. She founded a religious order and built this church.

Chapel Ste-Marguerite Bourgeoys picked the site for the chapel in 1657, just outside Ville-Marie's stockade. She persuaded Montréal's founder, Paul de Chomedey, to help with the project. The original building was destroyed by fire, and the present stone edifice dates from 1771. The 1998 renovation revealed some beautiful 18th-century murals.

A sailors' haunt The chapel has always been significant to mariners. Situated on the waterfront, it was built to house a small 17th-century statue of Notre-Dame-de-Bon-Secours (Our Lady of Good Hope), credited with the rescue of those in peril at sea. The late Montréal troubadour Leonard Cohen sang of the huge statue of the Virgin that graces the steeple of the present building, facing the river with arms outstretched, in his iconic song, "Suzanne". Mariners who survived ocean crossings in the 18th and 19th centuries often came to the church to thank the Virgin for her help, and to leave votive lamps in the shape of small model ships. Many of them still hang from the ceiling and the chapel is usually referred to simply as the Église des Matelots, the Sailors' Church. Visitors can climb the steeple to the "Aerial," a tiny chapel where mariners came to pray.

The Marché Bonsecours began life as a concert hall; now it's a shopping arcade

Marché Bonsecours

The silvery dome of the Marché Bonsecours is a landmark on the waterfront. Now housing art and crafts stores, it is a reminder of the city's importance as a busy port during the 19th century.

In the beginning The site of the Marché Bonsecours was important in 18th-century New France. Colonial authorities had an administrative center here and the Marché Neuf, built to replace Montréal's first market, was nearby. The British erected it between 1845 and 1850: The city councillors met downstairs and musicians played in the concert hall upstairs. It was only in 1878, when the mayor and city legislators moved to their new home on rue Notre-Dame, that it became a market and remained so until the early 1960s. After redevelopment, the building served again as municipal offices until May 1996, when it reopened as a shopping arcade.

Today The greystone building houses artists' and artisans' boutiques on the lower level, while the upper floor serves as a space for temporary exhibitions, concerts and banquets. One of the most graceful buildings in the city, its long neoclassical facade, punctuated by rows of white-painted sash windows, stretches for two blocks. The main portico, supported by six cast-iron Doric columns, fronts onto cobbled rue Saint-Paul in the heart of the old city. The back door opens on the Vieux-Port (▷ 32). In summer there is an outdoor café at street level.

THE BASICS

marchebonsecours.qc.ca

🔲 G10

✉ 350 rue Saint-Paul Est at rue Bonsecours

☎ 514/872-7730

🕐 Daily from 10am. Individual store opening times vary

🚇 Champ-de-Mars

🚌 14

♿ Very good

🎟 Free

HIGHLIGHTS

● Silver dome
● Facade and portico
● Shopping

TIPS

● For coffee, pastries, sandwiches or a light meal accompanied by wine or beer, visit Le Café des Arts inside the market.
● The Québec Craft Council's Boutique des Métiers d'Art is one of the 15 stores inside specializing in high-quality art and design items.

VIEUX-MONTRÉAL TOP 25

Place d'Youville

THE BASICS

ville.montreal.qc.ca
✚ F12
✉ 335 place d'Youville
☎ 514/872-3207
🕐 Tue–Sun 10–5
Ⓢ Square-Victoria, Place d'Armes
🚌 14, 55, 129
♿ Moderate
❓ Guided tours need to be arranged in advance

The fish market and dried-up creek are long gone, and what we see today is a public space that has been imaginatively landscaped.

History Place d'Youville is one of Montréal's earliest market squares, although it is actually a long, thin rectangle that has been extensively remodeled in recent time. Of the monuments and historic sites that line the square, the most attractive is the beautifully restored red-stone Caserne Centrale de Pompiers, or old Central Fire Station (1903). Today the building houses a history museum. While the museum may seem a little dated at first glance, it tells Montréal's story, from 1642 to the present, in an interesting way, using dioramas, videos and other media to trace the city's development

The peaceful Place d'Youville

from Iroquois settlement to metropolis. Look for the mock-ups of the streetcar, the 19th-century factory and the gaudy 1940s living room. Temporary exhibitions on offbeat aspects of the city's history are held upstairs.

HIGHLIGHTS

- Fire station building
- Tram car
- Youville Stables

Also on the square On the square's south side are the Youville Stables (Écuries d'Youville), graystone buildings constructed in 1828 as warehouses for grain merchants and soap manufacturers (the stables were next door). In 1967 the complex was converted into offices, shops and artisans' studios. Just off the square a plaque commemorates the Hôpital Général des Sœurs-Grises (Gray Nuns' General Hospital), founded in 1694 and taken over in 1747 by Marguerite d'Youville, the widow who founded the Sœurs Grises.

Pointe-à-Callière

Musée d'Archéologie et d'Histoire de Montréal has put Pointe-à-Callière well and truly on the map

THE BASICS

pacmusee.qc.ca

F11

350 place Royale

514/872-9150

Late Jun–Aug Mon–Fri 10–6, Sat–Sun 11–5, Sep–late Jun Tue–Fri 10–5, Sat–Sun 11–5

L'Arrivage Café-Restaurant

Place d'Armes

55, 61

Very good (uneven floor downstairs)

Expensive; free tours

HIGHLIGHTS

● Archaeological site
● Pirates or Privateers?
● Youville Pumping Station
● Where Montréal Was Born
● Multimedia show

TIPS

● Allow 1–2 hours for a visit.
● Admission includes free 20- or 60-minute guided tours (Tue–Sun only) in French and English.

Of all the innovations in the Vieux-Port, the superb Musée d'Archéologie et d'Histoire de Montréal at Pointe-à-Callière is the most impressive.

Archaeology and history Expanded in time for Montreal's 375th birthday in 2017, this museum should be your first stop to understand its evolution. It provides a fascinating introduction to the city's history: Pointe-à-Callière was where Montréal's first 53 settlers landed from France on May 17, 1642. Using audiovisual displays and light-and-sound shows, the museum tells the story of Montréal's development as a trading and meeting place.

Underground The main pavilion of this newly expanded museum is the stark, shiplike Édifice de l'Eperon. It houses offices, temporary exhibits, a café with river views and a theater with a 16-minute multimedia show on Montréal's history. But its real treasures are underground. The museum gives access to the excavations underneath, where archaeologists have burrowed into the silt and rock to expose the remains of a 19th-century sewer system, 18th-century tavern foundations and a cemetery dating back to 1643. As you explore, you have virtual encounters with some of the city's citizens. Tunnels connect the excavations to the Old Customs House, where there are more exhibits. The museum also incorporates the Youville Pumping Station, the city's first electrical wastewater-pumping system.

This graceful street, with its wide sidewalks, is a delightful place to stroll day and night

This cobblestone street is the picturesque main thoroughfare of Vieux-Montréal and dates from the origins of the city. Today its old buildings offer an enticing mix of art and craft galleries, shops, restaurants and boutique hotels.

Historic origins The street is named for Paul de Chomedey, founder of the city. Most of the old buildings that line the street date from the 19th and early 20th century and are a pleasing mix of stone and brick. The clever use of street lighting to highlight the architectural features makes an after-dark stroll doubly worthwhile. Daytime attractions include the Marché Bonsecours (▷ 27), the Chapelle Notre-Dame-de-Bon-Secours, with its Musée Marguerite-Bourgeoys (▷ 26), and the beautifully restored Maison Papineau (▷ 36), all clustered around the intersection with rue Bonsecours.

Vibrant street The real joy of rue Saint-Paul, though, is just to wander, explore the galleries and boutiques and soak up the atmosphere—which is particularly busy after dark or during any of the festivals based here or on the water-front, which runs parallel. It's also fun to join the locals on the roof terrace of the chic Hôtel Nelligan (▷ 112), a prime city spot for *cinq a sept* (5–7pm), the traditional Montréal after-work get-together. You can also hop over one street to the waterfront quays of the Vieux-Port (▷ 32), where there are facilities for many outdoor activities.

THE BASICS

☩ G11
Ⓜ Champ de Mars, Place d'Armes
🚌 55, 129

HIGHLIGHTS

● Marché Bonsecours
● The commercial art galleries
● A caleche ride (from place d'Armes)
● Bar-hopping after dark

Vieux-Port

TOP 25

Bassin Bonsecours, Prom du Vieux-Port

THE BASICS

oldportofmontreal.com
vieux-montreal.qu.ca
⊞ G11
⊠ Access from points along rue de la Commune and rue Berri
☎ 514/496-7678 or 800/971-7678
🍴 On Place Jacques-Cartier and elsewhere
Ⓜ Place d'Armes, Champ-de-Mars, Square-Victoria
🚌 55, 75, 715
♿ Free but fees for most attractions and ice rink

HIGHLIGHTS

● Centre des Sciences
● Labyrinthe du Hangar 16
● Centre d'Histoire de Montréal
● Tour de l'Horloge
● Multimedia show

TIPS

● Check the Old Port website for special offers.
● Free WiFi is available through most of the Old Port Area.

The Old Port was the heart of the city from its earliest days, home to the quays that received the first pioneers. The port was moved in 1976 and the area revitalized in the 1990s to create a dynamic waterfront that stretches for over a mile (2km) along the Saint Lawrence.

Leisure activities Attractions are divided between the park area set back from the water and the various old docks and piers and their converted warehouses. Among other things, the latter contain the Centre des Sciences de Montréal (▷ 33) and Labyrinthe du Hangar 16 (▷ 35), as well as providing the start point for many of the boat trips up and down the Saint Lawrence River (▷ 33). The waterfront park area is a pleasure to wander for its own sake, with plenty of trails, cafés and restaurants, most with outdoor terraces. You can also rent bikes, inline skates, pleasure boats and Segways to explore both this area and farther afield along the Lachine Canal at the port's eastern end.

Festivals In summer you'll always find a festival of some sort in progress, as well as street performers and bigger shows. In 2012 an urban beach was created near the Tour de l'Horloge (clock tower), begun in 1919 as a memorial to Canadian sailors who died in World War I—climb the tower for fine views. Winter, too, has its festivals, along with the chance to go ice fishing and join the locals skating on a large ice rink between December and early March.

More to See

BANQUE DE MONTRÉAL

Canada's oldest financial institution was founded in 1817. Thirty years later its headquarters moved to this neoclassical building inspired by Rome's Pantheon. The bank's small museum displays coins, mechanical piggy banks and a check written on a beaver pelt.

➕ F11 ✉ 129 rue Saint-Jacques ☎ 514/877-6810 🕐 Mon–Fri 9–4 🚇 Place d'Armes ♿ Good 🎟 Free

BOAT TRIPS ON THE SAINT LAWRENCE RIVER

The Saint Lawrence (Fleuve St.-Laurent) has been Montréal's lifeblood, a vital artery for trade and communication, for centuries. You can enjoy a taste of the great river on one of the short cruises or thrilling jet boats that leave from the Vieux-Port. Daytime and evening cruises are available, including dinner and entertainment cruises. Most offer views of the port area and islands of Notre-Dame and Sainte-Hélène, while a few venture farther afield to the Commune, Sainte-Marguerite and other islands beyond Longueuil.

➕ G10/G11 🚇 Champ-de-Mars, Place d'Armes 🚌 55, 129

Le Bateau Mouche
✉ Quai Jacques-Cartier ☎ 514/849-9952; bateaumouche.ca

Saute Moutons
✉ Quai de l'Horloge ☎ 514/284-9607; jetboatingmontreal.com

Croisières AML
✉ Quai King Edward ☎ 866/856-6668; croisieresaml.com

CENTRE DES SCIENCES DE MONTRÉAL

montrealsciencecentre.com
On one of the quays of the Vieux-Port, this excellent science museum offers exciting exhibits and interactive displays. It ranges from basic scientific concepts to the impact of science and technology on our daily lives, offers glimpses into the future and explores pressing ecological issues. There's the opportunity to create, edit and present your own

View of the Biosphère from a Bateau Mouche

Banque de Montréal

TV news segment and learn about the latest Canadian inventions and innovations. Sharing the building is an IMAX movie theater.

➕ G11 ✉ King Edward Pier, rue de la Commune ☎ 514/496-4724 or 877/496-4724 🕐 Mon–Fri 9–4, Sat–Sun 10–5 🚇 Place d'Armes 🚌 14, 55, 129 🍴 Café Arsenik 💰 Expensive; combined tickets with IMAX available

CHÂTEAU RAMEZAY

chateauramezay.qc.ca

With its squat round towers and its rough stone finish, Château Ramezay, commissioned by Claude de Ramezay, 11th Governor of Montréal, is one of North America's most venerable buildings. Sold in 1745 to the governors of the Compagnie des Indes (West Indies Company), the chateau was French Montréal's most fashionable meeting place before serving as official residence to the Governors General of British North America, military headquarters for American commanders Benedict Arnold and Richard Montgomery, and finally, in its present incarnation, as a museum.

Château Ramezay is much more than an opulently furnished historic house, however, with collections amounting to some 30,000 objects—fine arts, First Nations and colonial items, numismatics, photographs and a library. The gardens are dotted with information panels and often host special events.

➕ G10 ✉ 280 rue Notre-Dame Est at rue Saint-Claude ☎ 514/861-3708 🕐 Jun to mid-Oct daily 10–6; mid-Oct to May Tue–Sun 10–4.30 🚇 Champ-de-Mars 🚌 14, 129 💰 Moderate

ÉDIFICE ALDRED

Built in 1928, the Aldred Building (sometimes known as Édifice La Prévoyance), celebrated for its art deco features, is considered Montréal's original skyscraper. Despite its 23 stories towering over the older historic structures surrounding the Place d'Armes, the grey limestone building blends in

The Château Ramezay is a reminder of Normandy in North America

well with its environment. It is still used as offices so is not generally open to the public; however, try to have a peek at the opulence of the travertine, marble and bronze reception area and corridors.

➕ F11 ✉ 501–507 place d'Armes 🚇 Place d'Armes

HABITAT '67

Habitat '67 is a modern housing development designed for Expo '67 by Moshe Safdie, one of Montréal's leading architects. Safdie was disillusioned with suburbia and most public housing, especially high-rise developments, which he felt cut people off from open spaces and the amenities of the city. His project here was an attempt to build better housing more cheaply by mass-producing much of each housing unit in factories and then delivering them ready-made to the building's site. From afar, the project, with its cubist houses stacked on top of one another, looks strange and impressive but Montréalers never really

took to the dull concrete exteriors and inadequately protected pedestrian streets, and in 1986 the government sold the complex to its residents for just half the initial cost of $22 million.

➕ H12 ✉ avenue Pierre-Dupuy, Cité du Havre 🚌 168

LABYRINTHE DU HANGAR 16

soslabyrinthe.com

Both fun and educational, this indoor maze challenges children to hunt for clues and historical treasures while finding their way through the labyrinth. There's a different themed mystery to solve each year, centred on the maritime heritage of the area, in addition to specials such as a spooky Halloween event. Children under 13 must be accompanied, so adults get to join in the hunt too.

➕ G10 ✉ Quai de l'Horloge, Vieux-Port ☎ 514/499-0099 🕐 Mid-May–June 23 Sat–Sun and holidays 10–8; Jun 24–late Aug Mon 12–10, Tue–Sun 10–10; Sep–Oct daily 11–5.30 🚇 Champ-de-Mars 💰 Expensive

The strange box-like residential block (Habitat '67) built for Expo '67

LIEU HISTORIQUE NATIONAL SIR GEORGE-ÉTIENNE CARTIER

pc.gc.ca/lhn-nhs/qc/etiennecartier.aspx

Sir George-Étienne Cartier, once a leading rebel against British rule, was later to become one of the founding fathers of the Canadian confederation, persuading the French Canadians that a united Canada was the way forward. This museum occupies two connected houses that were home to the Cartier family between 1848 and 1872. One has displays explaining Cartier's political and industrial pre-occupations (he was a lawyer and the Grand Trunk Railway was one of his clients), while the other portrays his family life, complete with many original pieces of furniture and other domestic objects.

🏛 G10 ✉ 458 rue Notre-Dame Est, corner of rue Berri ☎ 514/283-2282 or 888/773-8888 🕐 Early Jun to early Sep daily 10–5; early Apr to early Jun, early Sep to Dec 23 Wed–Sun, holidays 10–5 🚇 Champ-de-Mars 🚌 14, 239 🎫 Inexpensive; theatrical presentations moderate ❓ Guided tours

MAISON PAPINEAU

This beautiful house was built by John Campbell, a colonel in the British army, who is said to have purchased the land from Joseph Papineau, the grandfather of Louis-Joseph Papineau (1786–1871), one of the great political figures in the French-Canadian nationalist movement. Campbell's widow then sold the house to Louis-Joseph's father, who in turn left it to Louis-Joseph, and it remained in the family until 1964. Today, it is owned by the Canadian government. The house has been restored to its splendid 1830s appearance as a memorial to Papineau. While the house in Old Montréal cannot be visited by the public, the Manoir Papineau, the home of Louis-Joseph Papineau in Montebello, Québec, an hour from the national capital of Ottawa, is a museum open to the public.

🏛 G10 ✉ 440 rue Bonsecours ☎ None 🕐 Exterior only 🚇 Champ-de-Mars ♿ On a sloping, cobbled street

Maison Papineau on rue Bonsecours

Inside Sir George-Étienne Cartier's former home

MAISON PIERRE-DU-CALVET

www.pierreducalvet.ca

This fine 18th-century greystone, built in 1770 for merchant Pierre du Calvet, is currently under renovation, with plans to open as a luxury boutique hotel with restaurant, bar, café-pâtisserie, and outdoor terrace in summer 2018.

🔁 G10 ✉ 401 rue Bonsecours
☎ 514/282-1725 🔲 Champ-de-Mars

PLACE D'ARMES

Place d'Armes was laid out at the end of the 17th century around the main source of drinking water for the first French settlement. In the center is a statue (1895) of Paul de Chomedey, Montréal's founder, Sieur de Maisonneuve. Around it are Basilique Notre-Dame (▷ 24–25), Montréal's oldest building, the Séminaire de Saint-Sulpice, the Banque de Montréal (▷ 33), the Aldred Building (▷ 34–35) and the eight-floor Édifice New York Life (1888).

🔁 F11 🔲 Place d'Armes

PLACE JACQUES-CARTIER

Right in the heart of Vieux-Montréal, this lovely cobbled square was created in 1804 as a municipal market; now its cafés, musicians, restaurants and quaint shops draw lively summer crowds, and in winter there's a small Christmas market where visitors can grab a wooden chair and warm up with a hot drink by one of the wood-burning stoves. An 1809 Nelson's Column is here and there are also several fine 19th-century houses, including the Maison del Vecchio, Maison Cartier and Maison Vandelac.

🔁 G10 🔲 Champ-de-Mars

PLACE ROYALE

Place Royale is Montréal's oldest square, and has a history that stretches back to when the area's aboriginal population occupied the site. Artifacts suggest the area has been continually inhabited for at least 2,000 years. For a period in the 17th century the site was used for an annual fur-trading market.

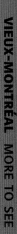

Place d'Armes

Place Jacques-Cartier

Thus was born the industry that would be the basis of Montréal's wealth for decades. In 1701, the French and aboriginal peoples signed a treaty here that brought an end to their wars. In later years the square was the site of public punishments, and was known then as Customs Square. It took its present name in 1892.

🔲 F11 🚇 Place d'Armes

RUE BONSECOURS

After visiting Marché Bonsecours (▷ 27), take a stroll down the adjoining street. It's a good example of the classical ideals of Montréal's early French planners, with fine homes that display architectural fashions from the 17th to the 19th centuries. Look for the recently renovated No. 401 Maison Pierre-du-Calvet (▷ 37) and No. 440 Maison Papineau (▷ 36). It also provides picturesque views of nearby Chapelle Notre-Dame-de-Bon-Secours.

🔲 G10 🚇 Champ-de-Mars

RUE SAINT-AMABLE

This narrow cobbled alley off place Jacques-Cartier is flanked by imposing stone houses, restaurants, shops and warehouses. It is just 5 metres (16.5 feet) wide on average, which adds to its busy atmosphere in summer. It is notorious for the many portrait artists vying for business amid the throng, although the local paintings and crafts on display are as likely to catch the eye of passersby.

🔲 G11 🚇 Place d'Armes

VIEUX PALAIS DE JUSTICE

The impressive neoclassical courthouse (1856) heard civil cases for over a century, although it was never quite large enough to fulfil its purpose and the court moved to a modern building in 1971. Most of it is now municipal offices, but you can admire the fine exterior features—the dome, fluted Ionic columns and portico.

🔲 F10 ✉ 155 rue Notre-Dame Est
🚇 Champ-de-Mars

Marché Bonsecours

Vieux Palais de Justice

Vieux-Montréal

This easy walk takes you along the main streets and past the key churches, monuments, squares and civic buildings of Old Montréal.

DISTANCE: 3km (2 miles) **ALLOW:** 2–6 hours depending on sights visited

START

PLACE JACQUES-CARTIER (▷ 37)
🚇 Place Jacques-Cartier 🚇 Champ-de-Mars

END

PLACE JACQUES-CARTIER

❶ Start at the northern end of place Jacques-Cartier beside the Admiral Lord Horatio Nelson's monument and walk east along rue Notre-Dame Est.

❷ Continue on rue Notre-Dame Est past Hôtel de Ville on the left. Visit the Château Ramezay (▷ 34) on the right and the Lieu Historique National Sir G.-É. Cartier (▷ 36).

❸ After the Lieu Historique National Sir G.-É. Cartier, backtrack and turn left on rue Berri and right on rue Saint-Paul Est, Canada's oldest commercial street.

❹ Pass the Maison Pierre-du-Calvet (▷ 37) on the right and Chapelle Notre-Dame-de-Bon-Secours (▷ 26) and Marché Bonsecours (▷ 27) on the left.

❽ Turn left on rue de la Commune Ouest to visit the Musée d'Archéologie et d'Histoire (▷ 30). Continue along the waterfront until you reach the southern end of place Jacques-Cartier.

❼ Visit Place d'Youville (▷ 28–9) and, if you have time, drop into the nearby Youville Stables (Écuries d'Youville).

❻ After passing the Séminaire de Saint-Sulpice turn left down rue Saint-François-Xavier, past the Old Stock Exchange (now the Centaur Theatre). Go right on rue Saint-Paul Ouest and left on rue Saint-Pierre to place d'Youville (▷ 28).

❺ Continue on rue Saint-Paul until you reach the bronze sculpture of the three ladies on the right. Turn right on rue Saint-Dizier, left at cours le Royer and right onto rue Saint-Sulpice to the Basilique Notre-Dame (▷ 24–25). Go left on rue Notre-Dame.

Shopping

BOUTIQUE DENIS GAGNON

denisgagnon.ca

An icon on the Montréal fashion scene, Denis Gagnon is known for his precise cuts, his couture approach to leather, and his airy silk pieces. His creations have even been exhibited at the Montréal Museum of Fine Arts. This boutique showcases his couture designs along with his prêt-à-porter collection.

➕ F11 ✉ 170B rue St-Paul Ouest ☎ 514/935-6360 🕐 Mon–Fri 11–5, Sat 11–6, Sun 12–5 🚇 Place d'Armes or Square-Victoria

BOUTIQUE U&I

boutiqueuandi.com

Fashionable boutique with trendsetting outerwear labels from North America and Europe, with an emphasis on Québec and Canadian brands such as Cydwoq, Canada Goose and Montréal label Mackage—designer of Meghan Markle's coat on her first official walkabout with fiancé Prince Harry.

➕ F11 ✉ 215 rue St-Paul Ouest ☎ 514/508-7704 🕐 Mon–Fri 10–7, Sat 9–7, Sun 9–6 🚇 Place d'Armes or Square-Victoria

CANADIAN MAPLE DELIGHTS

mapledelights.com

Mouthwatering aromas are overwhelming in this shop and bistro, where you can sample or buy a wide range of maple syrup-based products, including some pastries and delicious ice creams.

➕ G11 ✉ 84 rue Saint-Paul Est ☎ 514/765-3456, Ext 224 🕐 Mon–Thu 9–7, Fri 9–9, Sat 10–9, Sun 10–7 🚇 Champ-de-Mars

LE CHARIOT MÉTIERS D'ART

galeriesmontreal.ca/le-chariot-metiers-dart

A piece of Inuit or other aboriginal art is a distinctive and purely Canadian souvenir. This gallery has one of Canada's largest collections of soapstone, ivory and jade Inuit carvings, as well as numerous other high-quality works of art. Prices are correspondingly high.

➕ F11 ✉ 446 place Jacques-Cartier ☎ 514/875-6134 🕐 Daily 10–6 🚇 Champ-de-Mars 🚌 38

L'EMPREINTE COOPÉRATIVE

lempreintecoop.com

A dazzling store that showcases the work of numerous craftspeople from across the province of Québec. Browse everything from toys to homewares.

➕ G10 ✉ 88 rue Saint-Paul Est ☎ 514/861-4427 🕐 Sun–Wed 10–6, Thu–Sat 10–9 🚇 Place d'Armes

ESPACE PEPIN HOME

thepepinshop.com

Recently expanded, Espace Pepin is a designer's dream. An eclectic mix of high-end housewares, art and furniture, as well as clothing, apothecary products and accessories. The shop also houses a small café serving sandwiches and pastries.

➕ F12 ✉ 378 rue St-Paul Ouest ☎ 514/844-2512 🕐 Mon–Sat 10–6, Sun 11–5 🚇 Square-Victoria

---

SWEET SOUVENIRS

If you're looking for a souvenir to take home, think maple. Québec produces more than two-thirds of the world's supply of maple syrup. So valuable is this liquid gold that, between 2011 and 2012, maple syrup worth $18 million was stolen from a Québec warehouse. Not surprisingly, the stuff is ubiquitous on Montréal breakfast tables, and confectionery, butter and sugar made from maple sap are common treats. The best time to buy is in spring when the supply is plentiful. Best prices are at farmers' markets.

FLUEVOG

fluevog.com

John Fluevog has cultivated a loyal following in Canada for unconventional, yet top-quality shoes, distinguished by unusually curved lines and wonky heels.
➕ F11 ✉ 180 rue St-Paul Ouest
☎ 514/379-1970 🕐 Mon–Wed 11–7, Thu–Sat 11–8, Sun 12–6 🚇 Square-Victoria or Place d'Armes

GALERIE D'ART ÉMERAUDE

galerieemeraude.com

This specializes in Québécois and Canadian art, including the works of British-born painter Michael Foer, who was inspired by the Group of Seven (the Algonquin Group), whose landscape paintings launched the first major Canadian national art movement.
➕ F10 ✉ 301 rue St-Paul Est ☎ 514/845-2121 🕐 Mon–Sat 10–6, Sun 10–5
🚇 Champ-de-Mars

NOËL ETERNEL

noeleternel.com

It's always Christmas here, with a great variety of high-quality ornaments, decorations and collectible items—all designed for the festive season.
➕ F11 ✉ 660A Notre-Dame ☎ 514/285-4944 or 888/595-4944 🕐 Jan–Apr daily 10–5, May–Dec daily 10–6 🚇 Place d'Armes

PHILIPPE DUBUC

dubucstyle.com

Philippe Dubuc is one of Canada's premier designers of men's and women's clothes. This stylish boutique is his headquarters and displays both collections.
➕ E11 ✉ 417 rue St-Pierre, suite 101
☎ 514/282-1465 🕐 Mon–Wed 11–6, Thu–Fri 11–7, Sat 10.30–5, Sun 12–5 🚇 Square-Victoria

POINTE-À-CALLIÈRE

pacmuseum.qc.ca

For a superior memento of the city, visit this museum gift shop in the Ancienne-Douane (Old Customs) building. It has an excellent selection of books on art and local history and archaeology, pieces of First Nations art, craft items and reproduction artifacts from Québec and around the world.
➕ G11 ✉ 150 rue Saint-Paul Ouest
☎ 514/872-9150 🕐 Tue–Sun 11–6 🚇 Place d'Armes

ROONEY

rooneyshop.com

This is a fashionable clothing store/art gallery, with works by internationally known artists on vast exposed-brick walls. Clothing lines include Ella Moss, Hudson, Rocksmith, Yumi Kim, Casette, Corpus and many more.
➕ F12 ✉ 395 rue Notre-Dame Ouest
☎ 514/543-6234 🕐 Mon–Wed 11.30–6, Thu–Fri 11.30–8, Sat–Sun 12–5 🚇 Square-Victoria

RUE SAINT-PAUL

This street is home to a variety of stores, but is worth visiting for its art galleries and craft shops. Browse the high-quality work by local and other Québécois artists and craftspeople.
➕ G10–11 ✉ Rue Saint-Paul
🚇 Champ-de-Mars

STEVE'S MUSIC STORE

stevesmusic.com

This large and rambling store on the fringes of Vieux-Montréal is a magnet for musicians of every stripe, offering instruments, sheet music, songbooks and musical accessories.
➕ F11 ✉ 51 Saint-Antoine Ouest
☎ 514/878-2216 🕐 Mon–Wed 9–6, Thu–Fri 9–9, Sat 9–5, Sun 12–5 🚇 Place d'Armes

Entertainment and Nightlife

BATEAU MOUCHE DINNER CRUISE

bateaumouche.ca

Cruise with fabulous views of the river and the city and dine on a gourmet feast, accompanied by live music—usually either jazz or waltzes.

🔒 G11 ✉ Quai Jacques-Cartier ☎ 514/849-9952 or 800/361-9952 🕐 Mid-May to mid-Oct daily, departing at 7pm; duration 3.5 hours 💰 Expensive 🚇 Champ-de-Mars

CENTAUR THEATRE

centaurtheatre.com

The city's foremost English-language theater has a grand setting in the former Stock Exchange Building.

🔒 F11 ✉ 453 rue Saint-François-Xavier ☎ 514/288-3161 🚇 Place d'Armes

LES 2 PIERROTS

2pierrots.com

A crowded and convivial venue devoted to Québécois folk music. Performances are on the terrace in fine weather.

🔒 G11 ✉ 104 rue Saint-Paul Est ☎ 514/861-1270 🕐 Fri–Sat from 8.30pm 🚇 Place d'Armes

IMAX

centredessciencesdemontreal.com

If you like big-screen movies, this is the place, in the same building as the Centre des Sciences.

🔒 G11 ✉ Quai King-Edward ☎ 514/496-4724 or 877/496-4724 🕐 Daily from 10am; last screening begins 8pm 🚇 Place d'Armes

MODAVIE

modavie.com

The restaurant here is good for Mediterranean dishes and other stand-ards, but most people come for the large central bar, and for the live music, for which there is no cover charge.

There's a good choice of malts and cigars, and bar snacks are free during Happy Hour on weekdays.

🔒 G11 ✉ 1 rue Saint-Paul Ouest ☎ 514/287-9582 🕐 Mon–Thu 11.30–10.30, Fri 11.30–11, Sat noon–11, Sun noon–12.30am; live music Sun–Wed 8–10pm, Thu–Sat 7–11pm 🚇 Place d'Armes

PUB ST-PAUL

pubstpaul.com

The chief charms of this airy and friendly pub, with its rustic brick walls, flagstone floors and wooden beams, are its position close to the river and the views. It offers reasonable food, a wide range of beers and live music Friday and Saturday night.

🔒 G11 ✉ 124 rue Saint-Paul Ouest ☎ 514/874-0485 🕐 Mon–Fri 11.30am–3am, Sat–Sun noon–3am 🚇 Place d'Armes

VELVET SPEAKEASY

velvetspeakeasy.ca

An intimate and fun club set a block back from the waterfront. The music is mostly electro with the odd serving of pop and disco.

🔒 G10 ✉ 426 rue Saint-Gabriel ☎ 514/878-9782 🕐 Tue–Sun 10pm–3am 🚇 Place d'Armes

---

CIRQUE DU SOLEIL

This circus has come a long way since it was founded on the quays of Montréal's Old Port waterfront in 1984. Its dance, acrobatics, costumes and drama has made it an international success. It has resident companies in Las Vegas and elsewhere, and its international headquarters in Montréal, where new recruits train. Performances are staged in the blue-and-yellow tents on the Vieux-Port quayside (☎ 514/790–1245; cirquedusoleil.com).

Where to Eat

PRICES

Prices are approximate, based on a
3-course meal for one person.

\$\$\$	over \$45
\$\$	\$25–\$45
\$	under \$25

AUBERGE LE SAINT-GABRIEL ($$$)

aubergesaint-gabriel.com

This venerable inn is said to be the old-est in North America. Enjoy French and Québécois cooking in the large dining rooms or on the terrace.

🔲 G11 ✉ 426 rue Saint-Gabriel
☎ 514/878-3561 🕑 Apr–Aug daily lunch and dinner; Sep–Mar Tue–Fri lunch and dinner, Sat dinner 🚇 Place d'Armes

BONAPARTE ($$$)

restaurantbonaparte.com

Sit in the fireplace room overlooking rue Saint-Sacrement and you'll swear you're in Paris. The food is French, too.

🔲 F11 ✉ 443 rue Saint-François-Xavier
☎ 514/844-4368 🕑 Mon–Fri lunch and dinner, Sat–Sun dinner 🚇 Place d'Armes

BORIS BISTRO ($$)

borisbistro.com

Mostly gluten-free French bistro food–such as homemade sausage or braised rabbit—served on a delightful tree-shaded terrace.

🔲 F12 ✉ 465 rue McGill ☎ 514/848-9575
🕑 May–Sep daily lunch and dinner; Oct–Apr Mon–Fri lunch and dinner 🚇 Square-Victoria

CAFÉ STASH ($$)

restaurantstashcafe.ca

A Montréal institution, here you sit on pews to consume robust and warming Polish dishes—hot borscht, pierogi and several kinds of sausage.

🔲 G11 ✉ 200 rue Saint-Paul Ouest
☎ 514/845-6611 🕑 Daily lunch, dinner
🚇 Place d'Armes

CHEZ L'ÉPICIER ($$$)

chezlepicier.com

Fresh market cuisine served in the surroundings of an old grocery store offers unusual variations on French dishes. Try the sweetbreads braised in apple juice and fresh thyme.

🔲 G10 ✉ 311 rue Saint-Paul ☎ 514/878-2232 🕑 Tue–Sat dinner 🚇 Champ-de-Mars

CLUB CHASSE ET PECHE ($$)

leclubchasseetpeche.com

With just a coat of arms announcing its presence, this secretive little place is well worth seeking out for the deli-ciously imaginative food, with equally engaging menu descriptions.

🔲 G11 ✉ 423 rue St-Claude ☎ 514/861-1112 🕑 Tue–Sat dinner 🚇 Champ-de-Mars, Place d'Armes

DA EMMA ($$$)

Stone-walled basement room of a former women's prison, this iconic Montréal restaurant fills every one of its 130 seats even after 25 years in busi-ness. It is renowned for simple yet perfect Roman Italian fare.

🔲 G12 ✉ 777 rue de la Commune Ouest
☎ 514/392-1568 🕑 Mon–Fri lunch and dinner, Sat dinner 🚇 Square-Victoria

WORLD FLAVORS

Greek and Italian restaurants are endur-ingly popular in the city and Cantonese cooking has been a presence since the late 1800s. Refugees from Indochina in the 1970s opened Vietnamese restaurants and noodle shops. Thai food and sushi is also popular across the city.

GRAZIELLA ($$–$$$)

restaurantgraziella.ca

Simple northern-Italian dishes with a flair for presentation. A first course of feather-light ricotta gnocchi will not dull your appetite for hearty mains.

🚹 F12 🖂 116 rue McGill 🕿 514/876-0116 🕔 Tue–Fri lunch, dinner, Sat dinner 🚇 Square-Victoria

THE HAMBAR ($$$)

hotelstpaul.com or hambar.ca

The restaurant of the boutique Saint Paul Hotel (➤ 112) serves bold, market cuisine to a fashionable crowd.

🚹 F12 🖂 355 rue McGill 🕿 514/879-1234 🕔 Mon–Fri lunch, dinner, Sat–Sun dinner 🚇 Square-Victoria

INVITATION V ($$)

invitationv.com

An industrial-chic vegan restaurant where diners can enjoy organic dishes. Wine lovers can also sip guilt-free as the wines are produced without animal fining agents.

🚹 F10 🖂 201 rue St-Jacques 🕿 514/271-8111 🕔 Mon–Fri lunch, dinner, Sat–Sun brunch, lunch, dinner 🚇 Place d'Armes

LOV ($$$)

lov.com

LOV (local, organic, vegan) serves gourmet vegan and vegetarian cuisine, natural, biodynamic wines, organic beers, and botanical cocktails in lush, ethereally green and white settings.

🚹 F12 🖂 464 rue McGill 🕿 438/387-1326 🕔 Mon–Wed 11.30–10, Thu–Fri 11.30–11, Sat 10–11, Sun 10–10 🚇 Square-Victoria

OLIVE ET GOURMANDO ($)

oliveetgourmando.com

A superb bakery and eatery that offers soups, salads, panini and delicious hot or cold sandwiches with generous fillings, with gluten-free options.

🚹 G11 🖂 315 rue Saint-Paul Ouest 🕿 514/350-1083 🕔 Daily 9–5 🚇 Place d'Armes

LE PETIT DEP ($)

An adorable gourmet grocer and café serving third-wave coffee, prêt-à-manger soups, salads and comfort foods such as vegan shepherd's pie, along with delicious homemade sweets.

🚹 F11 🖂 179 St-Paul Ouest 🕿 514/ 284-9162 🕔 Daily 8am–11pm 🚇 Place d'Armes

TATAMI ($$)

This is an ideal place to stop on a tour of Vieux-Montréal. Grilled, spicy beef, salmon, chicken and squid are served in lacquered boxes along with salad and sticky rice.

🚹 F11 🖂 140 rue Notre-Dame Ouest 🕿 514/845-5864 🕔 Mon–Fri lunch, dinner, Sat dinner 🚇 Place d'Armes

TOQUE! ($$$)

restaurant-toque.com

Toque! has been one of Montréal's gastronomic temples for years, and its contemporary French and Asian fusion food has lost nothing over the time. It's the first choice for a treat.

🚹 F11 🖂 900 place Jean-Paul-Riopelle, near rue Saint-François-Xavier 🕿 514/499-2084 🕔 Tue–Fri lunch and dinner, Sat dinner 🚇 Place d'Armes

---

POPULAR MESS

Québec's own contribution to fast-food culture is something called *poutine* (literally "mess"). It consists of a huge plate of French fries, covered liberally with lumps of pale yellow cheese curds and drowned in thick, brown gravy.

Lovely churches, venerable museums and peaceful squares sit beside glittering sky-scrapers, dramatic art galleries and busy shopping streets, while beneath is another world entirely, the Underground City.

Cathédrale Marie-Reine-du-Monde

The huge copper cupola (right) and intricate statues atop the Cathédrale (left)

THE BASICS

cathedralecatholiquede
montreal.org

➕ E12

✉ 1085 rue de la
Cathédrale

☎ 514/866-1661

🕐 Mon–Fri 7–7, Sat–Sun
7.30–7. Closed during
services

Ⓟ Bonaventure

🚌 107, 150, 410, 420,
535

♿ Very good, but a steep
ramp

✋ Free

HIGHLIGHTS

● Stained glass
● High altar
● Bourget Chapel

Mary Queen of the World Cathedral brings a taste of the Italian Renaissance into the heart of Montréal.

St. Peter's in miniature Bishop Ignace Bourget, who began the cathedral three years after Canadian confederation, intended to underline papal supremacy and show that Catholicism still dominated what was then the largest city in the Dominion. So he set the cathedral, which is a one-quarter-size replica of St. Peter's in Rome, at the heart of the city's Anglo-Protestant district. Begun in 1870, the building was completed in 1894. Pope John-Paul II visited the cathedral during his pilgrimage to Canada in 1984.

Step inside In contrast to the lovely intimacy of Notre-Dame in Vieux-Montréal, the interior is somber, although the interiors of both churches are the work of architect Victor Bourgeau. The gloom was intended to intensify the effect of candles and accentuate the rose windows. The opulent high altar features a copy of the vast *baldacchino*, or altar canopy, by Bernini in St. Peter's, while the first little chapel in the left aisle has a red-flocked sanctuary filled with medals and saintly relics. Bishop Bourget is interred in a second chapel on the same side of the church, his recumbent figure surrounded by the tombs of his successors. On a pillar facing the bishop's tomb is a memorial to the men from the diocese who served in the Papal Zouaves in the fight against Italian nationalists.

Centre Canadien d'Architecture

There's something fitting about the layout of what is arguably the world's premier architectural museum. Its shape embraces an impressive 19th-century mansion.

Temple of architecture The gray limestone facade is long, low and virtually windowless, and the front door, at the building's western end, appears an afterthought. But that door leads into six beautifully lit halls given over to changing exhibits ranging from the academic to the whimsical—displays on modernist theory and American lawn culture are equally at home. Incorporated into the complex is the 1877 Shaughnessy Mansion, with its art nouveau conservatory, built for Canadian Pacific Railway chairman Sir Thomas Shaughnessy. Across the street, in an island of green between two busy main thoroughfares, is a garden designed by Melvin Charney, where fanciful fragments tell the story of architecture.

Phyllis Lambert The woman behind all this is architect Phyllis Lambert, a defender of Montréal's architectural heritage, who founded the center in 1979 and presided, with architect Peter Rose, over the building of its present home (1985–89). She also contributed her own impressive collection, now expanded to 100,000 prints and drawings (some by Leonardo da Vinci and Michelangelo), 55,000 architectural photographs and 200,000 books and publications dating from 15th-century manuscripts to the present.

THE BASICS

cca.qc.ca

➕ D14

✉ 1920 rue Baile, between rues Saint-Marc and du Fort

☎ 514/939-7026

🕐 Wed–Sat 11–6

Ⓜ Guy-Concordia (St. Mathieu exit)

🚌 15, 150

♿ Excellent

💲 Moderate (free with a weekly or monthly transit pass)

❓ Excellent bookstore

HIGHLIGHTS

● Facade
● Halls
● Mansion
● Conservatory
● Gardens

Christt Church Cathedral

Inside the cathedral (left); a skyscraper towers over the spire (right)

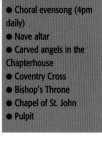

Surrounded on all sides by skyscrapers, the simple beauty and serenity of Christ Church Cathedral, with its steep timber ceiling and pointed arches, are a welcome respite from the bustle of downtown life.

A downtown haven Reminiscent of a 14th-century neo-Gothic English church, the city's Anglican cathedral was built between 1857 and 1859. The steeple was too heavy for the soft, unstable ground, and was replaced in 1927 with one made of aluminum plates, which were doctored to match the stone of the rest of the church. Among the notable objects inside is a cross (left and above the pulpit) made from nails rescued from the bombed Coventry Cathedral in England.

Money matters The seat of Montréal's Anglican bishop is a graceful ship of serenity floating on a sea of commerce. There are department stores on either side of it, a skyscraper behind and a shopping mall right underneath. Over time these soaring towers dwarfed the cathedral, while high maintenance costs and dwindling congregations led to a budgetary shortfall. The Anglican authorities found an imaginative solution in 1985 when they leased the land around and beneath the cathedral to developers. The church now sits atop Les Promenades Cathédrale (▷ 63), a busy mall. Shoppers, office workers and store clerks of all faiths retreat to the cathedral at midday for free concerts and organ recitals.

The building is contemporary (left), as are the works of art inside (right)

Musée d'Art Contemporain

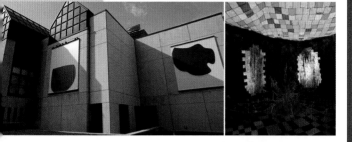

The stark, modern building of Montréal's museum of contemporary art is impressive, from its offbeat doors to the angular galleries and central atrium.

On the move Founded in 1964 by the Québec government, the museum occupied three different buildings before moving into its present home, only a stone's throw from Place des Arts. It originally focused on the work of indigenous Québécois artists, but the museum has increasingly widened its scope and mounts temporary exhibitions by artists from around the world.

The paintings Works in the gallery date from around 1939 up to the present, with at least 60 percent of the more than 5,000 works of art in the museum's collection by Québécois artists. Among those represented are David Moore, Alfred Pellan and Jean-Paul Riopelle, and there are 75 paintings by Montréal artist Paul-Émile Borduas. Other Canadian artists include Jack Bush, Michael Snow and Barbara Steinman. Works by Picasso, Lichtenstein and Warhol are also on display. Media includes video, sound and digital. Much of the permanent collection is often moved out to make way for temporary exhibitions, such as the hyperrealist portraits of Winnipeg artist Karel Funk, photographic creations by Brazilian Vik Muniz or the Thomas Hirschhorn installations *Jumbo Spoons* and *Big Cake*. Remember to look round the sculpture garden.

THE BASICS

macm.org

+ E10

✉ 185 rue Sainte-Catherine Ouest at rue Jeanne-Mance

☎ 514/847-6226

🕐 Tue 11–6, Wed–Fri 11–9, Sat–Sun 11–6

🍴 Le Contemporain

🚇 Place-des-Arts

🚌 15, 55, 80, 129, 535

♿ Very good

💲 Expensive; half-price Wed from 5pm

❓ Guided tours, live music events and children's activities

HIGHLIGHTS

● Architecture
● *Lips*, Geneviève Cadieux
● Steel atrium
● Sculpture garden
● *L'Île fortifiée*, Paul-Émile Borduas

DOWNTOWN TOP 25

51

McGill University

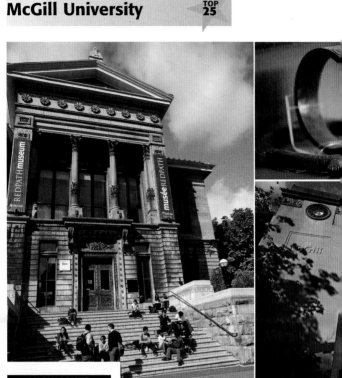

HIGHLIGHTS

- Roddick Gates
- Green space
- Redpath Museum
- Views
- Arts Building

TIPS

- Once the Redpath Library reading room, the Romanesque-style Redpath Hall now hosts music recitals and receptions.
- One of the most beautiful spaces on campus is the Gothic-inspired Octagon Room of the library of the Islamic Studies Institute.

Attractive architecture defines this fine university on the lower slopes of Mont-Royal, along with one of Canada's oldest and most eclectic museums. It's a privileged place from which to view the city.

Urban country The university opened in 1821 on a patch of pasture donated for the purpose by fur trader and land speculator James McGill. Since then, Montréal has spread northwards and now surrounds the 32ha (80-acre) campus. A great deal of green space is preserved within the boundaries of the university, including the lower field in the mid-campus area, where students can be seen studying, playing sports or just chilling out on sunny days. The lawns near the Arts Building are also attractive, with fine old trees.

Clockwise from left: taking a break on the steps of Redpath Museum; an ornament from the Congo and an African sculpture; a view inside the museum; the Roddick Gates, at the university's main entrance

Architecture The Greek Revival Roddick Gates guard the main entrance to the university on rue Sherbrooke Ouest, and behind them a tree-lined avenue leads to the 1839 neoclassical domed Arts Building, the oldest building on campus, containing the Moyse Hall, a theater. Along the avenue's east side are two further fine neoclassical buildings designed by Sir Andrew Taylor in the 1890s; he also designed the Library, with its elaborate carvings. Percy Nobbs's 1908 Macdonald Engineering Building is in the English baroque revival style. The most beautiful structure on campus is the templelike Redpath Museum of Natural History. It houses a huge and wonderfully whimsical collection that includes dinosaur bones, old coins, African art and a shrunken head. Under the trees a bronze James McGill hurries across campus.

THE BASICS

mcgill.ca

✚ D11

✉ 859 rue Sherbrooke Ouest

☎ Welcome Centre 514/398-6555; Redpath Museum 514/398-4086, Ext 00549

🕐 Welcome Centre Mon–Fri 9–4; Redpath Museum Mon–Fri 9–5 during academic year

🚇 McGill

♿ Fair

🆓 Free

Musée des Beaux-Arts

A painting, Mah-Min (1848), by Paul Kane (left) displayed in the museum (right)

THE BASICS

mbam.qc.ca

➕ C12

✉ 1379–1380 rue Sherbrooke Ouest

☎ 514/285-2000

🕐 Thu–Tue 11–5, Wed 5–9

🍴 Café des Beaux-Arts; also cafeteria

Ⓜ Guy-Concordia

🚌 24

♿ Good

🎟 Free permanent exhibition. Special shows expensive (half-price Wed 5–9)

HIGHLIGHTS

● *Portrait of a Young Woman*, Rembrandt
● *Portrait of a Man*, El Greco
● *Torso*, Henry Moore
● *October*, James Tissot
● *Automatic paintings*

Canada's oldest art museum consists of fine buildings facing each other across rue Sherbrooke Ouest, housing the country's best collection of Canadian paintings, as well as First Nations artifacts and old masters.

A fine museum This venerable institution is one of North America's finest galleries. The main building is unmistakable, with its stolid Vermont marble front and four large columns. Across the street stands the Desmarais Pavilion, a stunning modern building designed by Montréal architect Moshe Safdie.

The collection Canadian paintings range from works imported by the French settlers through to those by the Toronto-based Group of Seven. There are also period furnishings, drawings, engravings, silverware and art from ancient China, Japan, Egypt, Greece and South America. Among the old masters are works by Rembrandt and El Greco; Picasso, Henry Moore and Impressionists represent more recent eras.

Further expansion In 2011 the Erskine and American Church at the corner of rue Sherbrooke and Avenue du Musée became the Claire and Marc Bourgie Pavilion, housing the museum's vast collections of Canadian art, and in 2016 the Michal and Renata Hornstein Pavilion for Peace became home to 800 works, including 77 works of 17th-century Dutch and Flemish art.

Musée McCord d'Histoire Canadienne

A totem pole (left) and a sculpture by Dave McGary (2005; right) in the museum (middle)

The McCord Museum of Canadian History possesses a huge range of objects, including from Native Canadian culture, offering an insight into Montréal's past.

Bigger and bigger Montréal lawyer David Ross McCord (1844–1930) was a collector with an insatiable appetite for anything connected with Canadian history. In the 1920s he gave his huge collection of books, furniture, clothing, guns, paintings, documents, toys and photographs to McGill University, where it was housed in the McGill Union Building. The museum continues McCord's desire to present history to the nation.

Photographic collection The museum is strongest on the culture and history of Native Canadians, and includes some 16,600 costumes. Also remarkable are the Notman Photographic Archives, a collection of prints produced by photographic pioneer William Notman, who captured Victorian life in Montréal. The photographs include soldiers marching and members of the exclusive Montréal Athletic Association in snowshoes. Each of the hundreds of people shown in these pictures was photographed individually in the studio and then the photos were mounted onto an appropriate background. In all there are 450,000 photographs in the Archives, plus 800,000 images taken by other photographers. The museum also offers guided tours, a reading room and a documentation centre.

THE BASICS

mccord-museum.qc.ca
🔲 D11
✉ 690 rue Sherbrooke Ouest at rue Victoria
☎ 514/398-7100
🕐 Thu–Fri, Mon–Tue 10–6, Sat–Sun 10–5, Wed 11–9
🍴 The McCord Café
Ⓜ McGill
🚌 24, 125
♿ Good
💵 Expensive (free Wed 5–9)
❓ Guided tours, reading room

HIGHLIGHTS

● Notman Photographic Archives
● First Nations collection
● Historic prints and maps
● Decorative arts collection

Saint Patrick's Basilica

Stained-glass window (left); two apostles on the pulpit (middle); the lofty interior (right)

THE BASICS

stpatricksmtl.ca
✚ E11
✉ 454 boulevard René-Lévesque Ouest
☎ 514/866-7379
🕐 Mon–Fri 9 until end of 5.15 mass; Sat 10 until end of 5 mass; Sun 8.30 until end of 5 mass
🚇 Square-Victoria or McGill
♿ Fair
🎟 Free

HIGHLIGHTS

● Pulpit
● Sanctuary lamp
● Darcy McGee's pew

TIPS

● Take a break in the pleasant garden on the west side of the basilica.
● Hear the Saint Patrick's Basilica choir during the celebration of the Eucharist on Sunday at 11am September to June, in Latin every third Sunday of the month.

This graceful neo-Gothic building has a beautiful interior, with delicate mosaics and stained-glass windows that glow in the afternoon sunlight.

Our church Bishop Ignace Bourget gave only grudging approval when the Irish Catholics asked for a church of their own in 1843. The Mass, he reasoned, was in Latin, and most of the Irish spoke Gaelic at home so the Frenchness of the existing churches was immaterial. Still, Bourget saw no reason why they could not go to church with their French-speaking brethren. But the Irish community, who had mostly come to escape famine in their homeland, were adamant that they wanted their own place of worship, and with help from the Sulpician priests they erected a graceful neo-Gothic church.

Then there was light When the sun floods through the stained-glass figures of the four Evangelists, it fills the soaring nave with a honey glow. The vault over the sanctuary gleams with green and gold mosaics and the air smells of beeswax and incense. The pulpit and huge sanctuary lamp are highly decorated, painted panels line the walls of the nave and statues of bishops, martyrs, princesses and peasants jostle for space on the main altar and the niches of the side altars. Thomas Darcy McGee, one of the fathers of the confederation, was buried in Saint Patrick's after his assassination in 1868. His pew is marked with a Canadian flag.

Underground City

Shopping in Montréal's "Underground City" (left and right); 1000 de la Gauchetière (middle)

Harsh winters pale into insignificance in Montréal because of this vast Underground City. There are plenty of shops and restaurants, and easy access to those above ground, plus transportation links.

Beginnings Montréal's vast Underground City (officially known as RÉSO, from Réseau Piétonnier Souterrain) began in the early 1960s, when a mall full of shops and boutiques opened underneath the main plaza of place Ville-Marie, the city's first modern skyscraper. Both it and the neighboring Queen Elizabeth Hotel were built over the Canadian National Railway's tracks so it seemed natural enough to link both of them with Central Station, and to Place Bonaventure to the south. The idea really took off when the Métro opened in 1966.

Growth The underground now has more than 32km (20 miles) of wide, well-lit tunnels, mostly clustered around 10 of the Métro system's 68 stations. The system encompasses eight major hotels, two universities, both train stations, more than 1,700 boutiques, two department stores, more than 200 restaurants, at least 40 theaters and other entertainment venues, and the Centre Bell, but the only church with its own link to the system is Christ Church Cathedral. Bear in mind before venturing below ground that it's not always easy to navigate, so get a map and be prepared to ask the way. Remember that, while some are underground, most of the shops and malls are above ground.

THE BASICS

* E12
* Access at Métro stations in center
* Sun–Fri 5.30am–12.30am, Sat 5.30am–1am
* Peel, McGill, Bonaventure, Place-des-Arts, Square-Victoria
* Fair

HIGHLIGHTS

* Place Ville-Marie
* Les Halles de la Gare
* The ice rink at 1000 de la Gauchetière
* Centre CPD Capital and Terrasse du Parquet

More to See

AVENUE MCGILL COLLEGE
This short (four-block), wide boulevard runs from Cathcart near place Ville-Marie up to McGill University's Roddick Gates. If you stand on the place Ville-Marie plaza, you get a beautiful sweeping view of Mount Royal with its cross, and the campus framed by glass office towers. In summer, this is a great place to eat lunch outside one of the many cafés or restaurants, and to admire the annual photography exhibition curated by McCord Museum (▷ 55) on the west side of the avenue. Another artistic attraction is the striking sculpture group *The Illuminated Crowd* (▷ opposite).
⊞ D11 ⊚ McGill

RUE SAINTE-CATHERINE
Montréal's premier shopping street, rue Sainte-Catherine is also the longest commercial street in North America. Those with the stamina to walk its length would find its character changes along the way, as it passes through the Quartier Latin,

the Gay Village (simply known as the Village; ▷ 93) and Quartier des Spectacles. In some places it is classy and upscale. Elsewhere it is a honeypot of mainstream shopping, with all the familiar favorites. Between May and September many parts of the street are pedestrian-only and provide the stage for a wide variety of festivals and events through the year, not least Le Festival International de Montréal en Arts (mtlenarts.com), when "BoulevArt" turns a long section of the street into eastern Canada's largest outdoor art gallery.
⊞ D12 ⊚ Peel, McGill

RUE SHERBROOKE
This grand thoroughfare cuts across Montréal island and, at 31km (19 miles), it is the second-longest street in Montréal after boulevard Gouin. The section in this downtown area includes the classiest shopping. The street's most interesting section flanks the area known as the Golden Square Mile,

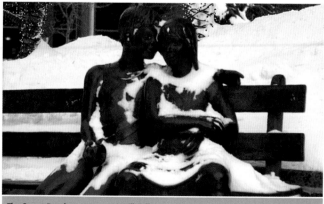

The Secret Bench *on avenue McGill College*

Montréal's most opulent district in the late 19th century, which runs from north to south between avenue des Pins to René-Lévesque boulevard and west to east between rue Guy/Chemin Côtedes-Neiges, and boulevard Robert-Bourassa/rue Université. Although shops still line the street, and you'll still find many international names in luxury and fashion, it is no longer the exclusive domain of the luxury retailers that once catered to the district's wealthy mansion owners.

🔒 D11 🚇 Peel, McGill

SQUARE PHILLIPS

An immense statue of King Edward VII, sculpted by Philippe Hébert in 1914, dominates this pleasant open space on rue Sainte-Catherine, named after building contractor Thomas Phillips. In summer street vendors' stands and market stalls compete with the square's shops. Note the 1921 Canada Cement Building, designed by the same architects as the Aldred Building (▷ 34), and not only the first office building to be built from reinforced concrete but also the first in Montréal to have its own underground parking garage.

🔒 E11 🚇 McGill

TOUR BNP-BANQUE LAURENTIENNE

These twin 20- and 16-story blue-glass towers, housing the headquarters of the Laurentian Bank, are eye-catching on the downtown skyline, dominating a particularly pleasant stretch of avenue McGill. The sculptural group *The Illuminated Crowd*, in front of the towers, is one of Montréal's most photographed exterior artworks. Raymond Mason's 65 larger-than-life white figures represent a cross-section of people and symbolize the fragility of humanity. They create a stunning contrast to the towers' blue-tinted glass.

🔒 D11 ✉ 1981 avenue McGill College 🚇 McGill

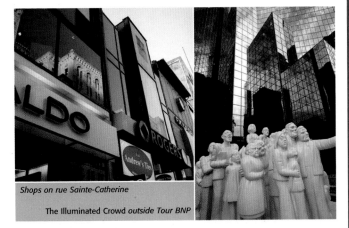

Shops on rue Sainte-Catherine

The Illuminated Crowd *outside Tour BNP*

Heart of Downtown

At street level this walk explores the dazzling high-rise heart of the modern city above the underground in the Cité Souterraine.

DISTANCE: 3km (2 miles) **ALLOW:** 1.5 hours

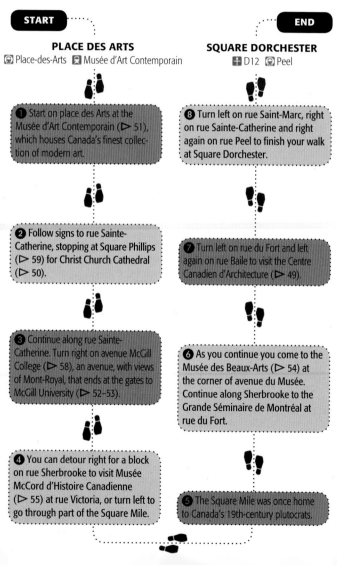

START

PLACE DES ARTS
🚇 Place-des-Arts 🏛 Musée d'Art Contemporain

END

SQUARE DORCHESTER
✚ D12 🚇 Peel

① Start on place des Arts at the Musée d'Art Contemporain (▷ 51), which houses Canada's finest collection of modern art.

② Follow signs to rue Sainte-Catherine, stopping at Square Phillips (▷ 59) for Christ Church Cathedral (▷ 50).

③ Continue along rue Sainte-Catherine. Turn right on avenue McGill College (▷ 58), an avenue, with views of Mont-Royal, that ends at the gates to McGill University (▷ 52–53).

④ You can detour right for a block on rue Sherbrooke to visit Musée McCord d'Histoire Canadienne (▷ 55) at rue Victoria, or turn left to go through part of the Square Mile.

⑧ Turn left on rue Saint-Marc, right on rue Sainte-Catherine and right again on rue Peel to finish your walk at Square Dorchester.

⑦ Turn left on rue du Fort and left again on rue Baile to visit the Centre Canadien d'Architecture (▷ 49).

⑥ As you continue you come to the Musée des Beaux-Arts (▷ 54) at the corner of avenue du Musée. Continue along Sherbrooke to the Grande Séminaire de Montréal at rue du Fort.

⑤ The Square Mile was once home to Canada's 19th-century plutocrats.

Shopping

ALAN KLINKHOFF GALLERY

klinkhoff.ca

The Klinkhoffs have been selling fine Canadian art such as the works of Tom Thompson, one of Canada's legendary Group of Seven, Charles Gagnon and William Kurelek since 1949.

🔲 C12 ✉ 1448 rue Sherbrooke Ouest ☎ 514/284-9339 🕐 Sep–May Tue–Sat 9–5, Jun–Aug Mon–Fri 9–5 🚇 Guy-Concordia

LA BAIE D'HUDSON (HUDSON'S BAY)

thebay.com

The Hudson's Bay Company, founded in 1891, still sells the company's distinctive blankets, as well as the full range of usual department store goods.

🔲 E11 ✉ 585 rue Sainte-Catherine Ouest at Square Phillips ☎ 514/281-4422 🕐 Mon–Fri 10–9, Sat 9–8, Sun 10–7 🚇 McGill

LE CENTRE EATON

centreeatondemontreal.com

The venerable Canadian department store that gave this mall its name closed its doors in 1999 but the mall's five floors of boutiques and shops thrive.

🔲 E12 ✉ 705 rue Sainte-Catherine Ouest ☎ 514/288-3708 🕐 Mon–Fri 10–9, Sat 10–6, Sun 11–5 🚇 McGill

COMPLEXE DESJARDINS

complexedesjardins.com

This vast multitiered complex is the largest mall in downtown. In addition to about 100 shops you'll find bistros, restaurants, cinemas, offices and a large piazza used for cultural events. Fountains and exotic plants make the space very pleasant.

🔲 E10 ✉ 150 rue Sainte-Catherine Ouest at Saint-Urbain ☎ 514/281-1870 🕐 Mon–Wed 9.30–6, Thu–Fri 9.30–9, Sat 9.30–5, Sun 12–5 🚇 Place-des-Arts

FRANK AND OAK

frankandoak.com

This concept store covering three floors in downtown Montréal is popular for its affordable classic designs, monthly events like whisky tastings and its full-service barber shop.

🔲 D11 ✉ 1420 Stanley Street ☎ 514/228-3761 🕐 Mon–Wed 10–7, Thu–Fri 10–9, Sat 10–6, Sun 11–5 🚇 Peel

GALERIE ELCA LONDON

elcalondon.com

This is the only gallery in the city devoted to Inuit arts and crafts; some of the prices for the gallery-quality art and artifacts are prohibitive, but come anyway to admire what's on show.

🔲 C12 ✉ 1444 rue Sherbrooke Ouest ☎ 514/282-1173 🕐 Tue–Sat 10–5 🚇 Guy-Concordia

GUILDE CANADIENNE DES MÉTIERS D'ART

laguilde.com

You'll find Canadian crafts such as blown glass, porcelain, pewter, tapestry and jewelry, plus an exhibition of Inuit, First Peoples and Canadian artifacts.

🔲 C12 ✉ 1356 rue Sherbrooke Ouest ☎ 514/849-6091 🕐 Tue, Thu–Fri 10–6, Sat–Sun 10–5, Wed 10–9 🚇 Guy-Concordia

SHOPPING DISTRICTS

Montréal's busiest shopping revolves around rue Ste-Catherine. For luxury labels, head to Ogilvy and Holt Renfrew (soon to merge). West along rue Sherbrooke, discover exclusive galleries and antique shops. Vieux-Montréal shopping has become upscale, while vintage and design options proliferate in Mile End and the Plateau on boulevard Saint-Laurent, avenue Mont-Royal and rue Saint-Viateur.

HENRI HENRI

henrihenri.ca

This fine men's hat shop stocks everything from handwoven Panamas to jaunty berets and even baseball caps.

➕ F10 ✉ 189 rue Sainte-Catherine Est, corner of rue Hôtel-de-Ville ☎ 514/288-0109 or 888/388-0109 ⏰ Mon–Fri 10–6, Sat–Sun 10–5 Ⓜ Saint-Laurent, Berri-UQAM

OGILVY

ogilvycanada.com

Top names in homeware and fashion have their own little shops within this classy department store, along with the top-floor designer shops.

➕ D13 ✉ 1307 rue Sainte-Catherine Ouest ☎ 514/842-7711 ⏰ Mon–Wed 10–6, Thu–Fri 10–9, Sat 9.30–5, Sun 11–6 Ⓜ Peel

PARAGRAPHE BOOK STORE

paragraphbooks.com

Popular with serious book lovers and students, with lectures and readings by leading Canadian authors.

➕ D11 ✉ 2220 avenue McGill College ☎ 514/845-5811 ⏰ Mon–Fri 8am–9pm, Sat–Sun 9–9 Ⓜ McGill

LES PROMENADES CATHÉDRALE

promenadescathedrale.com

The five-layer vertical mall was created under Christ Church Cathedral, and includes 60 shops, boutiques, cafés and restaurants, all connected to the Underground City (▷ 57).

➕ E11 ✉ 625 rue Sainte-Catherine Ouest ☎ 514/845-8230 ⏰ Mon–Wed 10–6, Thu–Fri 10–9, Sat 10–5, Sun 11–5 Ⓜ McGill

ROOTS

roots.com

Roots is now a national institution, full of inexpensive and timeless clothes, shoes and home furnishings.

➕ D12 ✉ 1025 rue Sainte-Catherine Ouest ☎ 514/845-7995 ⏰ Mon–Wed 10–8, Thu–Fri 10–9, Sat 9–7, Sun 10–7 Ⓜ McGill, Peel

SIMONS

simons.ca

This small chain, which sells housewares and clothing for both men and women, has been owned by the same Québec City family since 1840.

➕ D12 ✉ 977 rue Sainte-Catherine Ouest ☎ 514/282-1840 ⏰ Mon–Wed 10–6, Thu–Fri 10–9, Sat 10–5.30, Sun 11–5.30 Ⓜ Peel

ULYSSES LA LIBRAIRIE DU VOYAGE

ulyssesguides.com

Travel books in French and English, as well as maps and travel-related artifacts.

➕ D11 ✉ 560 avenue du Président-Kennedy, near avenue Union ☎ 514/843-9447 ⏰ Mon–Wed 10.30–6, Thu–Fri 10–6.30, Sat 10–5, Sun 11–5 Ⓜ McGill

L'UOMO MONTRÉAL

luomo-montreal.com

Top-name European designer clothing, footwear and acccessories for men, with European-style tailors and expert wardrobe coordinators on hand to advise.

➕ D12 ✉ 1452 rue Peel ☎ 514/844-1008 or 877/844-1008 ⏰ Mon–Wed 9.30–6, Thu–Fri 9.30–7.30, Sat 9.30–5 Ⓜ Peel

MALL SHOPPING

Shopping in Montréal's malls is an all-season endeavor. Most of them are linked into the Underground City's (▷ 57) extensive network of tunnels and Métro lines. Many major department stores are connected to the system, and some have become mini-malls, opening shops within shops to showcase designers such as Jean-Claude Chacok, Guy Laroche and Cacherel.

Entertainment and Nightlife

CAFÉ-BAR SAINT-SULPICE

lesaintsulpice.ca

This is a favorite among students and is busy for its vast terrace and music.

🚩 E10 ✉ 1680 rue Saint-Denis ☎ 514/844-9458 🕐 Bar daily 3.30pm–3am; restaurant Thu–Sat from 5pm 🚇 Berri-UQAM

CENTRE BELL

centrebell.ca

The home of the Montréal Canadiens also hosts big-name rock concerts.

🚩 E13 ✉ 1260 rue de la Gauchetière Ouest ☎ 514/790-1245 🚇 Lucien-l'Allier, Bonaventure

CINÉMA BANQUE SCOTIA MONTRÉAL

Downtown center with 15 theaters—two with IMAX screens—that show films in French and English.

🚩 D12 ✉ 977 rue Sainte-Catherine Ouest ☎ 514/842-0549 🚇 McGill

CLUB LOUNGE KARINA'S

winniesbar.com

One of the biggest and slickest clubs on rue Crescent, offering a mix of live and recorded Latin, jazz, R&B and hip hop.

🚩 D12 ✉ 1455 rue Crescent ☎ 514/288-0616 🕐 Thu–Sat 8pm–3am 🚇 Guy-Concordia

COMEDY NEST

thecomedynest.com

Renowned comedy club hosting top-notch touring stand-up acts.

🚩 C14 ✉ Montréal Forum, 3rd Floor, rue Sainte-Catherine at Atwater ☎ 514/932-6378 🚇 Atwater

HOUSE OF JAZZ

houseofjazz.ca

A bar, a restaurant and one of the best venues in the city for live jazz and blues.

🚩 D11 ✉ 2060 rue Aylmer near rue Sherbrooke ☎ 514/842-8656 🕐 Mon 6pm–midnight, Tue–Thu 11.30am–11.30pm, Fri 11.30am–1.30am, Sat 6pm–1.30am, Sun 6pm–11.30pm 🚇 McGill

PLACE DES ARTS

laplacedesarts.com

Montréal's showcase for the performing arts has five major performance spaces and houses the Orchestre Symphonique de Montréal, Orchestre Métropolitain de Montréal, Opéra de Montréal and the city's principal ballet troupe. Call after 4pm for deeply discounted tickets to that evening's performance.

🚩 E10 ✉ 260 boulevard de Maisonneuve Ouest ☎ Information 514/285-4200, tickets 514/842-2112, toll-free 866/842-2112 🕐 Box office Mon–Sat 10–6 🚇 Place-des-Arts

PUB SIR WINSTON CHURCHILL

winniesbar.com

This is an English-style pub, known as "Winnies," with a dance floor.

🚩 D12 ✉ 1455–59 rue Crescent ☎ 514/288-3814 🕐 Daily 11.30am–3am 🚇 Peel, Guy-Concordia

PUB LE VIEUX DUBLIN

dublinpub.ca

A much-loved Irish pub that's especially popular on its live Celtic music, five nights a week.

🚩 E12 ✉ 636 rue Cathcart ☎ 514/861-4448 🕐 Mon–Sat 11am–3am, Sun 4pm–midnight. 🚇 McGill

SALSATHÈQUE

salsatheque.ca

Popular downtown Latin club offering live music in addition to house DJs.

🚩 D12 ✉ 1220 rue Peel at rue Sainte-Catherine Ouest ☎ 514/875-0016 🕐 Thu–Sun 9pm–3am 🚇 Peel

Where to Eat

BEAVER HALL ($$–$$$)

beaverhall.ca

Within days of opening, this restaurant became a firm favorite for its terrific atmosphere and great food, ranging from a succulent burger to artistically presented steak tartar.

🚹 E12 ✉ 1073 côte du Beaverhall ☎ 514/866-1331 🕓 Mon–Fri lunch and dinner, Sat dinner 🚇 Square-Victoria

BRUTOPIA ($–$$)

brutopia.net

This is a great brewpub, with three bars on three floors and terraces outside each. As well as the eight house beers, there's a satisfying menu of international treats, including spicy pan-fried dumplings, chorizo nachos and quesadillas.

🚹 D13 ✉ 1219 rue Crescent ☎ 514/393-9277 🕓 Daily 2pm–3am, Fri noon–3am 🚇 Lucien-L'Allier

CAFE BISTRO ($$)

mccord-museum.qc.ca

This is a chic spot in the McCord Museum serving seasonal Québec and European-inspired cuisine.

🚹 D11 ✉ McCord Museum of Canadian History, 690 rue Sherbrooke Ouest ☎ 514/398-7100 ext 306 🕓 Tue–Fri lunch 🚇 McGill

CAFÉ FERREIRA ($$$)

ferreiracafe.com

Haute cuisine Portuguese style. Nibble on salted cod and olives while you con-

sider the grilled octopus or the sausages marinated in red wine.

🚹 D12 ✉ 1446 rue Peel ☎ 514/848-0988 🕓 Mon–Fri lunch, dinner, Sat dinner 🚇 Peel ❓ Reserve ahead

L'ENTRECÔTE SAINT-JEAN ($$)

lentrecotestjean.com

Classic bistro decor featuring high ceiling, mirrored walls, close tables, with a simple and inexpensive menu emphasizing steak served with matchstick fries.

🚹 D12 ✉ 2022 rue Peel ☎ 514/281-6492 🕓 Mon–Fri lunch, dinner, Sat–Sun dinner 🚇 Peel

ESCONDITE CERVECERIA ($$)

escondite.ca

This stylish newcomer is known for its enticing drinks menu, its fresh, juicy tacos and its lively ambience. The guacamole is said to be the best in the city.

🚹 E11 ✉ 1206 Union Avenue ☎ 514/419-9755 🕓 Tue–Wed 11.30–2.30, 5.30–10, Thu–Fri 11.30–2.30, 5.30–11, Sat 5.30–11, Sun 5.30–10 🚇 McGill

LOV ($$–$$$)

lov.com

LOV, which stands for local, organic, vegan, serves gourmet vegan and

vegetarian cuisine, as well as natural biodynamic wines, organic beers and botanical cocktails in lush, ethereally green and white surroundings.

🔢 C12 ✉ 1232 rue de la Montagne ☎ 514/287-1155 🕐 Mon–Wed 11.30–10, Thu–Fri 11.30–11, Sat 10am–11pm, Sun 10–10 🚇 Guy-Concordia

LA MAISON V.I.P. ($$)

It's far from fancy and it doesn't take reservations, but this Chinatown restaurant serves generous portions of authentic Cantonese dishes to an appreciative crowd of locals who don't mind waiting in line.

🔢 F11 ✉ 1077 rue Clark ☎ 514/861-1943 🕐 Daily 11.30am–4am 🚇 Place d'Armes

MR. STEER ($)

mistersteer.com

A simple steakhouse with leatherette booths serving great burgers.

🔢 D12 ✉ 1198 rue Sainte-Catherine Ouest, corner of Drummond ☎ 514/866-3233 🕐 Daily lunch, dinner 🚇 Peel

ORCHIDÉE DE CHINE ($$$)

lorchideedechine.net

Best of the upscale Chinese restaurants, with the dishes you'd expect served in an elegantly simple setting.

🔢 D12 ✉ 2017 rue Peel ☎ 514/287-1878 🕐 Mon–Fri lunch, dinner, Sat–Sun dinner 🚇 Peel

PIZZERIA NO.900 ($$)

no900.com

Neapolitan pizza served in stylish surroundings, with vintage-style black and white floor tiles, elbow-to-elbow tables and a small open kitchen from which you can observe the *pizzaiolos* at work. The pizza is always perfect, the atmosphere lively and the wine list just right.

🔢 C11 ✉ 2049 rue Peel ☎ 514/303-0334 🕐 Mon–Wed 11–10, Thu–Fri 11–11, Sat 11.30–11, Sun 11.30–10 🚇 Peel

PRESSE CAFÉ ($)

pressecafe.com

Good coffee, baked goods, sandwiches and salads, in a bright, cheery setting.

🔢 D12 ✉ 1001 boulevard Maisonneuve Ouest ☎ 514/844-5999 🕐 Daily 6am–7pm 🚇 Peel

RUBY ROUGE ($$)

restaurantrubyrouge.com

This large Chinatown restaurant is popular with families, especially for dim sum.

🔢 F11 ✉ 1008 rue Clark ☎ 514/390-8828 🕐 Daily 8am–11pm 🚇 Place d'Armes

LE TAJ ($$)

restaurantletaj.com

North Indian specialties, including good tandoori and vegetarian options.

🔢 D12 ✉ 2077 rue Stanley, near blvd de Maisonneuve ☎ 514/845-9015 🕐 Sun–Fri lunch and dinner, Sat dinner 🚇 Peel

TANGIA ($$$)

tangia.ca

The atrium garden of this prettily decorated three-room Moroccan restaurant is the perfect place for couscous, *kefta*, *merguez* and fresh, exotic salads.

🔢 D12 ✉ 2072 rue Drummond ☎ 514/282-9790 🕐 Mon, Sat dinner, Tue–Fri lunch and dinner 🚇 Peel

---

CHEAP EATS

The food courts in the Centre Eaton, Gare Centrale, Complexe Desjardins and Place Ville-Marie are a cut above the usual. Here you'll find stalls selling pastries, Mexican food, sausages and smoked meat, as well as the expected chicken, burgers and fries.

A glorious park protects the heights of Mont-Royal, providing fine walks and sweeping views across the city. Between here and Parc Lafontaine are the Quartier Latin and other lively neighborhoods.

AVENUE PAPINEAU

Rue Fabre
Rue de Grandpré
anaudière
hambord
beuf
Rue Garnier
Bienville
EST
Avenue
Émile-Duployé

RACHEL

Parc
la Fontaine

SHERBROOKE EST

Pavillon
la Fontaine

AVENUE

Ruelle de Mentana
Rue Duluth
Saint-Christophe
Rue Chateaubriand

DU
PARC
Rue Napoléon
Roy
Rue
de

LAFONTAINE
EST Mentana
Saint-André
Bousquet
Cherrier

SAINT-HUBERT

AFONTAINE

SAINT-
théâtre
aujourd'hui

Berri
RRSSSMC
(Institut des
Sourdes-Muettes)
Sherbrooke

Studio de
l'Agora
de la Danse

DE NIS
Drolet

335

SAINT-JACQUES
Rue Saint-Christophe
RUE

Gare d'Autocars
de Montréal
Avenue
Rue

MAISONNEUVE EST

Rue St-Christophe

PINS
Roy

Square
Saint-Louis

SAINT-LOUIS

SHERBROOKE

Rue
Saint-Denis

ONTARIO
Bibliothèque
Nat

RUE

Berri-
UQAM
Savoie

Parc
Émile-
Gamelin
Rue Labelle

SAINT-HUBERT

Misericordia

AVENUE DES
Théâtre de
Quat' Sous
Coloniale
Rue Prince Arthur

Avenue de
Bullion
de

CÉGEP
du Vieux
Montréal

R. Emery
Cinémathèque
Québecoise

Berri
UQAM

Galerie de
l'UQAM

SAINTE-CATHERINE

Berri

SAINT-DENIS EST

Chapelle
Notre-Dame-
de-Lourdes

Théâtre
La Chapelle
Rue

BOULEVARD
Clark
Milton
Rue

SAINT-NORBERT
l'Hôtel-de-Ville

SAINT-LAURENT

**QUARTIER
LATIN**

Parc
Toussaint-
Louverture

BOULEVARD

Rue de Boisbriand
RUE

Sanguinet
Rue
Ste-Elisabeth

BOULEVARD RENÉ-LÉVESQUE EST

Rue de La Gauchetière Est

Hôpital
Saint-Luc

inte-Famille

D   **E**   **F**

Oratoire Saint-Joseph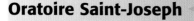

HIGHLIGHTS

- Oratory Museum
- The Primitive Chapel
- Joseph Guardo's eight bas-reliefs
- Gardens of the Way of the Cross

TIPS

- The Oratory Museum is open daily 10–4.30.
- The church has a good caféteria and gift shop.
- You may hear the Petits Chanteurs choir at services on Saturday and Sunday.

The dome of the Oratoire Saint-Joseph is a distinctive city landmark, and the church beneath it is the most important Roman Catholic shrine dedicated to Christ's earthly father.

Miracle cures The story begins with Brother André Bessette, a diminutive, barely literate man born in 1837 to a poor rural family. He joined the Congrégation de Sainte-Croix and worked as a porter in their college. He built a small shrine to his favorite saint and cared for sick pilgrims, gaining a reputation as a healer. Donations poured in from grateful pilgrims to help André fulfill his dream of building a grand monument to Saint Joseph. Construction began in 1924 but Brother André only lived long enough to see the completion of the crypt.

Clockwise from left: Oratoire Saint-Joseph is a striking landmark set against the blue sky; the Primitive Chapel; a sculpture in the Gardens of the Way of the Cross; a statue of the famed healer, Brother André, beneath the dome in the apse

Interior André was beatified in 1982 and buried in the oratory, which also includes part of his original chapel, a museum, the hospice room in which he died and his preserved heart. Climb to the observatory for a superb view, and to see the Carrara marble sculptures marking the Stations of the Cross in Mont-Royal.

Development Visitor numbers have increased to 2 million, and a massive renovation project is underway. Accessibility has been improved—escalators and an elevator have been installed and facilities have been adapted for wheelchair users and other visitors with reduced mobility. A "Holy Family Plaza," a multi-purpose, outdoor pedestrian area is planned, as well as a reconfiguration of the monument garden in front of the Oratory and an increase in green space.

THE BASICS

saint-joseph.org
- Off map at A13
- 3800 chemin Queen Mary, near Côte-des-Neiges
- 514/733-8211 or 877/672-8647
- Late Jun–Aug daily 6.30am–9.30pm; Sep–late Jun daily 7am–9pm
- Café
- Côte-des-Neiges
- 51, 165, 166
- Very good
- Oratory free. Museum guided tours inexpensive

Parc du Mont-Royal

TOP 25

HIGHLIGHTS

● Montréal Cross
● Le Chalet viewpoint
● Beaver Lake
● Smith House
● Mont-Royal Cemetery

TIP

● Energetic visitors can rent bicycles, skates, snowshoes, Nordic skis and kick-sleds, inner tubes (a bouncy alternative to toboggans) and pedal boats.

Mont-Royal's nickname is the "the Mountain," an appropriately grand title given the hold this steep, green oasis has on locals' affection.

Park on the hill Mont-Royal is one of seven peaks on the Saint Lawrence plain, all composed of intrusive rock hard enough to have survived the glacial erosion of the last Ice Age. Explorer Jacques Cartier named the hill—probably in honor of his royal patron, François I of France—on his first voyage up the Saint Lawrence in 1535. The area became a park in 1876, amid fears that the forested slopes were being denuded for firewood. The land was bought for $1 million, and landscaped by Frederick Law Olmsted, who was also responsible for New York's Central Park.

Clockwise from left: Beaver Lake, created in the 1930s; there are spectacular views of Montréal from Le Chalet, during the day or when the city lights come on; jogging along the shore of Beaver Lake

So much to do The park is too large to see in a day, so pick a corner to explore. Most people on foot enter at the Monument Sir George-Étienne Cartier, a popular summer venue for street musicians, vendors and people-watchers. Olmsted Road leads to the Montréal Cross on the summit. Beaver Lake, created in the 1930s, is another focal point, as is Le Chalet, which has fantastic views from its Belvédère Kondiaronk. The Smith House, dating from 1858, is the park's Welcome Centre, with an exhibition about the park's history and ecology, an information point, gift shop and café. There are two cemeteries on the northern edge that offer surprisingly pleasant strolls (look for the grave of Ann Leonowens, immortalized in *The King and I*, in the Mont-Royal Cemetery). In winter, rent skis, skates and snowshoes at the park.

THE BASICS

lemontroyal.qc.ca

✛ B11

✉ Entrances off avenue du Parc, avenue des Pins and elsewhere

☎ 514/843-8240

🕐 Park daily 6am–midnight; Smith House Mon–Fri 9–6, Sat–Sun 10–6 (winter hours vary)

🍴 The Chalet, Café Smith

🚇 Mont-Royal, then bus to top

🚌 11, 80, 129, 165, 535

♿ Some steep paths

🎟 Free

Plateau and Mile End

Bernard Street in the Mile End district (left); Bagels on sale (right)

THE BASICS

⊞ D7/B8
◎ Mont-Royal, Laurier

HIGHLIGHTS

- Vernacular architecture
- St.-Viateur Bagel bakery
- Avenue Mont-Royal
- Avenue Laurier

These neighborhoods are packed with individual boutiques and vibrant bars, restaurants and live music venues. On summer evenings the residential streets have a great buzz, with occupants socializing on their balconies.

Blue-collar origins Dating from the Industrial Revolution and originally built for working-class families, the two- or three-floor row-houses that line the streets contain separate apartments on each floor. Their outdoor staircases and balconies serve a dual purpose, giving each apartment a private external door and, with no need for internal staircases, providing more living space inside.

Plateau The Plateau lies north of rue Sherbrooke to the east of Parc du Mont-Royal. Its main commercial thoroughfares are avenue du Mont-Royal and rue Saint-Denis, both lined by individual boutiques and specialty stores, restaurants and cafés. Place Gérald-Godin is a lively spot, with street entertainers in summer.

Mile End Strictly part of the borough of Plateau-Mont-Royal, Mile End is quite distinct, more multicultural, more industrial and less prettified. It has attracted not only artists and musicians but also fashion and furniture designers, techies and computer graphics animators. The most chic shopping is around avenue Laurier and boulevard Saint-Laurent, again packed with one-of-a-kind stores.

More to See

CHAPELLE NOTRE-DAME-DE-LOURDES

cndlm.org

The Quartier Latin's Our Lady of Lourdes Chapel faces the old church of Saint-Jacques, hidden behind a bland exterior. But its sumptuously decorated interior, a mixture of Romanesque and Byzantine styles that dates from 1876, has vivid murals—the work of artist Napoléon Bourassa.

🚇 F9 ✉ 430 rue Sainte-Catherine Est ☎ 514/842-4704 🕐 Mon–Fri 11–6, Sat 10.30–6.30, Sun 9–6.30 🚊 Berri-UQAM

GALERIE DE L'UQAM

galerie.uqam.ca

This modern gallery was established as part of the Université du Québec à Montréal (UQAM) in 1975 with the collection from the former school of fine arts. It has expanded, but the emphasis is still on engaging students and visitors with a thought-provoking schedule of temporary exhibitions. The gallery mostly has contemporary art.

🚇 F9 ✉ Université du Québec à Montréal, 1400 rue Berri ☎ 514/987-6150 🕐 Tue–Sat 12–6 🚊 Berri-UQAM 🎟 Free

MUSÉE DES HOSPITALIÈRES

museedeshospitalieres.qc.ca

The museum tells the story of the Hôtel-Dieu, Montréal's first hospital, and the Hospitalières de Saint-Joseph, recruited in France in 1659 by Montréal's co-founder, Jeanne Mance. The displays also deal with the working lives of the medical staff there, their training and the treatments they administered, their religious inspiration and the history of medicine. There are also regular temporary exhibitions, which draw on aspects of the collection of 20,000 artifacts and documents held here to give a more general overview of the history of medicine.

🚇 D10 ✉ 201 avenue des Pins Ouest ☎ 514/849-2919 🕐 Mid-Mar to mid-Oct Tue–Fri 10–5, Sat–Sun 1–5; mid-Oct to mid-Dec Wed–Sun 1–5; groups only Jan to mid-Mar 🚊 Sherbrooke 🚌 144 🚻 Fair 🎟 Moderate

Chapelle Notre-Dame-de-Lourdes

PARC LAFONTAINE

This beautiful park is a large expanse of green within the Plateau neighborhood, and residents and visitors alike make full use of its many attractions. Its summer appeal is obvious, with its two linked ponds, lawns to lounge on, the cycle path and playing fields; in winter there's skating and hockey. Lafontaine divides into an English-style landscape in the west and a French-style garden in the east, with tennis courts, outdoor swimming pools and summer concerts.

➕ E7 ✉ avenue du Parc Lafontaine, between Sherbrooke Est and Rachel ⏱ Daily 9am–10pm 🍴 Snack bar 🚇 Sherbrooke 🚌 14, 24, 29 ♿ Good 💲 Free

RUE SAINT-DENIS

Rue Saint-Denis bisects Montréal's Latin Quarter and is a colorful and picturesque mix of interesting architecture and boutiques, some looking as if they occupy the front room of someone's house. Up outside staircases or dipping down into the basement of an old stone building, there's an appealing mix of haute-couture boutiques, designer homewares, individualistic music stores, antiques shops, arts, crafts and gifts. There are plenty of cafés, bistros and restaurants for weary shoppers. The nightlife is good here, too, with lots of bars and pubs, and there's also the Théâtre d'Aujourd'hui, which showcases cutting-edge works by Québec playwrights.

➕ E9 🚇 Berri-UQAM, Sherbrooke

SQUARE SAINT-LOUIS

This leafy square was laid out in 1879 and is considered one of the city's finest. Its beautiful houses— very French-looking—are now home to poets, artists and writers attracted by the bohemian atmosphere of the surrounding Latin Quarter. Despite hosting some of the most expensive real estate in the city, the park it surrounds attracts some eccentric characters.

➕ E9 🚇 Sherbrooke

The ponds at Parc Lafontaine

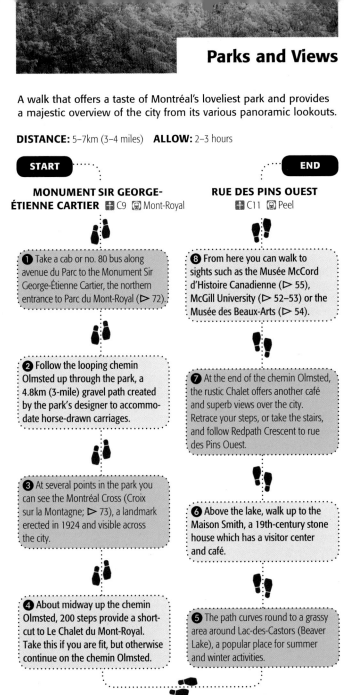

Parks and Views

A walk that offers a taste of Montréal's loveliest park and provides a majestic overview of the city from its various panoramic lookouts.

DISTANCE: 5–7km (3–4 miles) **ALLOW:** 2–3 hours

START

MONUMENT SIR GEORGE-ÉTIENNE CARTIER ✚ C9 Ⓜ Mont-Royal

END

RUE DES PINS OUEST ✚ C11 Ⓜ Peel

❶ Take a cab or no. 80 bus along avenue du Parc to the Monument Sir George-Étienne Cartier, the northern entrance to Parc du Mont-Royal (▷ 72).

❷ Follow the looping chemin Olmsted up through the park, a 4.8km (3-mile) gravel path created by the park's designer to accommodate horse-drawn carriages.

❸ At several points in the park you can see the Montréal Cross (Croix sur la Montagne; ▷ 73), a landmark erected in 1924 and visible across the city.

❹ About midway up the chemin Olmsted, 200 steps provide a shortcut to Le Chalet du Mont-Royal. Take this if you are fit, but otherwise continue on the chemin Olmsted.

❽ From here you can walk to sights such as the Musée McCord d'Histoire Canadienne (▷ 55), McGill University (▷ 52–53) or the Musée des Beaux-Arts (▷ 54).

❼ At the end of the chemin Olmsted, the rustic Chalet offers another café and superb views over the city. Retrace your steps, or take the stairs, and follow Redpath Crescent to rue des Pins Ouest.

❻ Above the lake, walk up to the Maison Smith, a 19th-century stone house which has a visitor center and café.

❺ The path curves round to a grassy area around Lac-des-Castors (Beaver Lake), a popular place for summer and winter activities.

Shopping

ARCHAMBAULT

archambault.ca

Montréal's own music and bookshop is excellent for current releases, classical music and Québec pop. It also has an extensive selection of song books and sheet music.

🔢 E10 ✉ 175 rue Sainte-Catherine Est ☎ 514/849-8589 🕐 Mon–Wed 8–6, Thu–Fri 8–9, Sat 12–6, Sun 12–5 🚇 Berri-UQAM

GENERAL 54

general54.ca

Accessories and jewelry designed and made by more than 30 designers and artists are showcased, including the clothing line of co-owner Jen Glasgow.

🔢 A7 ✉ 5145 Boul St.-Laurent ☎ 514/271-2129 🕐 Mon–Wed 11–6, Thu–Fri 11–8, Sat–Sun 11–5 🚇 Laurier

KANUK

kanuk.com

Here you can uncover everything you need for when the temperature drops. The coats, sleeping bags and gloves are widely available, but you'll find the keenest prices here at the factory store, where there is a big sale in November.

🔢 D8 ✉ 485 rue Rachel Est ☎ 514/284-4494 or 877/284-4494 🕐 Mon–Wed 10–6, Thu–Fri 10–9, Sat–Sun 10–5 🚇 Mont-Royal

ST-VIATEUR BAGEL

stviateurbagel.com

Established in 1957, this one of Montréal's landmark bagel bakeries. Shunning innovation, they have only ever made two varieties—sesame and poppy seed. Other branches, with cafés, are located at 1127 avenue du Mont-Royal Est and 5629 avenue Monkland.

🔢 A8 ✉ 263 avenue Saint-Viateur Ouest ☎ 514/276-8044 or 866/662-2435 🕐 Daily 24 hours 🚇 Laurier or Outremont

TONY PAPPAS

tonypappas.ca

Established in 1900, this shoe shop is a refreshing change from the chains downtown. It stocks international names and Québec-made styles. It also has a first-class traditional repair shop.

🔢 D6 ✉ 1822 avenue Mont-Royal Est ☎ 514/521-0820 🕐 Mon–Wed 8.30–6, Thu–Fri 8.30–9, Sat 8.30–5, Sun 12–5 🚇 Mont-Royal

VALET D'COEUR

levalet.com

This is a shop for children and adults of all ages, and sells an excellent range of board games, comics, posters and toys. Its range of chess sets and boards is second to none.

🔢 C8 ✉ 4408 rue Saint-Denis ☎ 888/499-5389 🕐 Mon–Wed 10–6, Thu–Fri 10–9, Sat 10–5, Sun 12–5 🚇 Mont-Royal

WAXMAN

waxman.ca

Long-established purveyor of formal menswear in a very elegant showroom. You can get made-to-measure or off-the-peg tuxedos, vests and accessories, or rent a suit if you need to.

🔢 B9 ✉ 4605 avenue du Parc ☎ 514/845-8826 🕐 Mon–Wed 9–6, Thu–Fri 9–9, Sat 9–4 🚇 Mont-Royal

---

WHERE TO LOOK

Antiques hunters can search for treasures in the lavish shops along rue Sherbrooke Ouest and in exclusive Westmount. More modest finds are on Antique Alley on rue Notre-Dame Ouest. Lovers of 20th-century vintage goods haunt rue Amherst, for wooden toys at Antiquités Curiosités at No. 1769, or scavenge for quirky post-1950s items at Boutique Spoutnik, at No. 2120.

Entertainment and Nightlife

APARTMENT 200

This loft-style space has a bar, video-gaming, DJs and dancing, fusing the home and bar into one space.

➕ D9 ✉ 3643 boulevard Saint-Laurent ☎ 514/282-7665 🕐 Daily 7pm–3am 🚇 Saint-Laurent

LE BALATTOU

balattou.com

Established for more than 30 years, this is a welcoming (if hot and crowded) club with an African and tropical motif. You can hear live world music several nights a week.

➕ C8 ✉ 4372 boulevard Saint-Laurent ☎ 514/845-5447 🕐 Tue–Sun 9pm–3am 🚌 29, 55

BILY KUN

bilykun.com

Come early evening to the Czech-inspired tavern whose name means white horse to hear jazz (Tue–Fri) or classical music (Sun) or, after 10pm any night, DJ music.

➕ C8 ✉ 354 avenue du Mont-Royal Est ☎ 514/845-5392 🕐 Mon–Sat 3pm–3am, Sun 3pm–midnight 🚇 Mont-Royal

BISTRO A JOJO

bistroajojo.com

A relaxed and intimate blues club that's been in business since 1975. Come early to be sure of one of the simple wooden chairs at the close-packed tables. Great people-watching on the sidewalk terrace.

➕ E9 ✉ 1627 rue Saint-Denis ☎ 514/843-5015 🕐 Daily noon–3am 🚇 Berri-UQAM

LE CHEVAL BLANC

lechevalblanc.ca

Unchanged for 25 years, music combines with the buzz of arty and political talk. Communal tables to share the artisan beer, brewed onsite.

➕ E9 ✉ 809 rue Ontario Est ☎ 514/522-0211 🕐 Daily 3pm–3am 🚇 Berri-UQAM

LE CLUB SODA

clubsoda.ca

This is an excellent venue where you can be sure to find good live music (including big international names) and other shows, such as comedy.

➕ E10 ✉ 1225 boulevard Saint-Laurent ☎ 514/286-1010 🕐 Daily 8pm–2am 🚇 Saint-Laurent

DIESE ONZE JAZZ CLUB

dieseonze.com

There's nightly live jazz, and often also an opener for the after-work crowd in this intimate basement. Tapas and light main plates are served, too, at reasonable prices.

➕ D8 ✉ 4115 rue Saint-Denis ☎ 514/223-3543 🕐 Daily from 5pm 🚇 Sherbrooke

MME LEE

A sleek contemporary lounge-club where music, numerous cocktails and tapas-style snacks combine to create a speakeasy atmosphere.

➕ E9 ✉ 151 rue Ontario Est ☎ 438/383-7673 🕐 Tue–Fri 5pm–3am, Sat 9pm–3am 🚇 Saint-Laurent

---

WHERE TO GO?

Clubs are notorious for fading in and out of fashion, or for closing down altogether, so for the latest on clubs check the free magazines to be found at tourist offices, record shops and cafés. *The Mirror, the Hour* and the French-language *Voir* (all free) contain extensive listings of clubs and live music venues, as does *The Montreal Gazette*, the city's main English-language newspaper.

Where to Eat

PRICES

Prices are approximate, based on a 3-course meal for one person.

$$$	over $45
$$	$25–$45
$	under $25

AU PIED DE COCHON ($$)

aupieddecochon.ca

Celebrity chef Martin Picard's unapologetically gluttonous meat-based dishes continue to please a select crowd.

🚉 D8 ✉ 536 avenue Duluth ☎ 514/281-1114 🕐 Wed–Sun dinner 🚇 Sherbrooke, Mont-Royal ❓ Reservations essential

BEAUTY'S ($)

beautys.ca

A Montréal fixture since 1942, original owner and family patriarch Hymie Sckolnick enthusiastically ran the iconic diner until his death, at 96, in December 2017. The line out the door can be daunting on weekends and the setting has barely changed since it opened, but patrons—locals, tourists and Hollywood royalty alike—come here for the memorable food and character, not the decor.

🚉 B8 ✉ 93 rue Mont-Royal Ouest ☎ 514/849-8883 🕐 Mon–Fri 7–3, Sat–Sun 8–4 🚇 Mont-Royal 🚌 80, 97

BISTROT LA FABRIQUE ($$$)

bistrolafabrique.com

Reserve a middle table to watch popular chef Jean-Baptiste Marchand and his team prepare your dinner in the very public kitchen. Don't miss his signature French toast for dessert, or try to choose from the long weekend brunch menu.

🚉 C8 ✉ 3609 rue Saint-Denis ☎ 514/544-5038 🕐 Tue–Fri dinner, Sat–Sun brunch, lunch, dinner 🚇 Sherbrooke

BON BLÉ RIZ ($$)

Don't be dissuaded by the facade or the interior decor; this longstanding Chinese restaurant on boulevard St.-Laurent has been serving a loyal Montréal clientele for the last 30 years. Popular dishes include lamb in a peppery anise-flavoured sauce, spicy shrimp, and pork and vegetables over crunchy home-made noodles with maple syrup.

🚉 E10 ✉ 1437 boulevard Saint-Laurent ☎ 514/844-1447 🕐 Tue–Fri lunch, dinner, Sat dinner 🚇 Saint-Laurent

CAFÉ SANTROPOL ($)

santropol.com

This is a bohemian student café with mainly vegetarian food. Attractions include more than 60 herbal teas, as well as a choice of ice creams, malts and sodas, and plenty of fruit juices, salads and quiches. In summer, the garden is a welcome retreat.

🚉 C9 ✉ 3990 rue Saint-Urbain ☎ 514/842-3110 🕐 Daily 11.30–10.30 🚇 Sherbrooke

L'EXPRESS ($$)

restaurantexpress.com

Iconic Parisian-style bistro with a zinc bar, elbow-to-elbow tables, cheerfully frantic service, perfect food and interesting wines.

🚉 D8 ✉ 3927 rue Saint-Denis at rue Duluth ☎ 514/845-5333 🕐 Mon–Fri 8am–3am, Sat 10am–3am, Sun 10am–2am 🚇 Sherbrooke ❓ Reservations essential

MOISHE'S ($)

moishes.ca

Eat marbled steak aged the same way since 1938 at this premier steak house, run by the same family of Jewish-Romanian descent since it opened. Its high standards ensure it's always crowded and noisy.

🕂 C9 ✉ 3961 boulevard Saint-Laurent at rue Duluth ☎ 514/845-3509 🕐 Daily dinner 🚇 Saint-Laurent, then bus 55 north

MOLESKINE ($$$)

moleskinerestaurant.com

One of the best restaurants to open in 2016, Moleskine is spread out on two floors. Downstairs is a casual space built around a wood-burning oven and open kitchen serving pizza, pastas and salads, while the upper floor serves more gastronomic fare. Decor is black-and-grey industrial chic, with chain-metal curtains and rough surfaces, and the chefs play vinyl records for that extra retro ambiance.

🕂 D10 ✉ 3412 avenue du Parc ☎ 514/903-6939 🕐 Tue–Sat 11–11 🚇 Place-des-Arts 🚌 80

OMNIVORE ($)

omnivoregrill.com

An informal counter-service restaurant with a Mediterranean and Middle Eastern flavor that offers excellent grilled and other meats (all organic), as well as snacks, sandwiches, specials up on the blackboard and a good choice for vegetarians and vegans (hence the name).

🕂 C9 ✉ 4351 boulevard Saint-Laurent at rue Marie-Anne ☎ 514/303-5757 🕐 Mon–Sat 11–10 🚇 Mont-Royal

PULLMAN ($$–$$$)

pullman-mtl.com

The first—and one of the best—wine bars in the city, Pullman impresses not only with its classy ambiance, its 300-plus wines and tasty nibbles, but also with its centerpiece, an enormous wine-glass chandelier.

🕂 D10 ✉ 3424 avenue du Parc ☎ 514/288-7779 🕐 Sun–Tue 4.30pm–midnight, Wed–Sat 4.30pm–1am 🚌 80, 24

SCHWARTZ'S ($)

schwartzdeli.com

The best thing on the menu is smoked meat but the steaks are pretty good too. Famous and packed, expect brusque service and lines.

🕂 D9 ✉ 3895 boulevard Saint-Laurent at rue Napoléon ☎ 514/842-4813 🕐 Sun–Thu 8am–12.30am, Fri 8am–1.30am, Sat 8am–2.30am 🚇 Mont-Royal

UNIBURGER ($)

uniburger.com

Uniburger's food has won plaudits, with fresh ingredients, a casual setting and a simple menu. It's popular with students.

🕂 E9 ✉ 302 rue Ontario Est ☎ 514/419-6555 🕐 Mon–Sat 11–9, Sun 12–8 🚇 Berri-UQAM

VEGANO ($)

veganomontreal.com

Montréal's first vegan Italian restaurant, opened in 2016, has weekly menus featuring plant-based breakfast and lunch dishes such as omelettes, pastas, creamy risottos, and baked goods such as almond croissants and chocolate cake. Bring your own wine.

🕂 D7 ✉ 432 rue Rachel Est ☎ 514/369-0000 🕐 Sat, Wed–Thu 9–3, Fri 9am–10pm 🚇 Mont-Royal

The striking stadium and buildings created for the 1976 Olympic Games, along with the Jardin Botanique, one of the world's largest botanical gardens, provide a great counterpart to Montréal's other attractions.

Maisonneuve and Le Village

Biodôme de Montréal

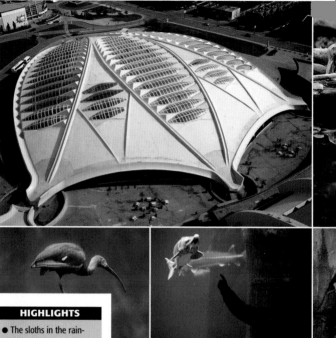

HIGHLIGHTS

● The sloths in the rainforest
● The beaver dam and lodge in the Saint Lawrence habitat
● Puffins and penguins in the Arctic and Antarctic areas

TIPS

● Use the free shuttle bus to travel between the Biodôme, Parc Olympique, Viau Métro, Insectarium and Jardin Botanique (mid-May to late October).
● Rent binoculars at the Biodôme for close-up views.

The Biodôme has been a success ever since it opened in 1992 in what used to be the Olympic velodrome. This living museum integrates birds, animals and plants into superb re-creations of their natural habitats.

Habitats Montréal's Biodôme replicates four beautiful habitats—tropical forest, the Saint Lawrence marine ecosystem, Laurentian forest, and the Arctic and Antarctic—with their plants, birds, marine creatures and other animals. You watch otters frolicking in waterfalls, observe marine creatures through glass and peek at animals and preening birds through the foliage of living forest. It is also actively involved in breeding endangered species in captivity with the hope of releasing the offspring into the wild.

Clockwise from left: Montréal's Biodôme contains four ecosystems; a visitor watches the fish; the huge globe provides a central point to touch base; a tamarin in the tropical forest; a penguin looks around; watching a fish in the Saint Lawrence marine ecosystem; a brightly colored resident of the tropical forest

Animals As you walk into the first habitat, the Amazonian rainforest, heat, humidity and animal smells hit you like a wall. Exotic birds chirp overhead, while the leafy undergrowth is alive with crocodiles, capybaras and golden lion tamarins (orange-furred monkeys that are increasingly scarce in their native Brazil). You'll also see darting parrots, a cave full of bats (behind glass) and other mammals, amphibians, reptiles and fish. A tank in the Saint Lawrence marine ecosystem recreates a sea, complete with nesting gannets and a tidal pool filled with sea urchins and anemones. There are popular puffins and penguins in the Arctic and Antarctic areas. Behind-the-scenes exhibits and events offer background into the scientific team's conservation, enhancement and development of living collections at the Biodôme.

THE BASICS

espacepourlavie.ca

🚼 G1

✉ 4777 avenue Pierre-de-Coubertin

☎ 514/868-3000

🕐 Closed for renovations in 2018. Check website for latest opening times

🍴 Café

Ⓥ Viau

♿ Very good

💰 Expensive. Combined tickets available with Jardin Botanique

❓ Gift shop

Jardin Botanique de Montréal

HIGHLIGHTS

● Summer butterflies
● Tropical greenhouse gardens (open year-round)
● Orchids and begonias
● First Nations Garden
● The Rose Garden
● The Chinese Garden

TIPS

● Check ahead for times of the tea ceremonies in the Japanese Garden Pavilion and the *Croque Insectes*.
● Leave enough time for the arboretum, as it covers a big area.

Montréal has the world's second-largest botanical gardens—no small feat given the cruel climate. The preserve is a blend of exotic horticulture with the beauty and tranquility of a formal garden.

Gardens Opened in 1931, Montréal's lovely botanical gardens comprise some 30 different outdoor gardens and 10 vast exhibition greenhouses. Each garden and glasshouse represents a different climate, country or style, ranging from a collection of poisonous plants to gardens devoted to orchids or medicinal herbs. Nearby lies the Insectarium, in a bug-shape building. Its galleries are filled with displays of countless insects living and dead (and exotic butterflies in summer). Don't miss the gargantuan South American cockroaches. In February

visitors can try some high-protein morsels as local cooks whip up chocolate-covered ants, honey-dipped bees and bug-centered lollipops.

Shanghai surprise The gardens' highlight is the 2ha (6-acre) Montréal-Shanghai Dream Lake Garden (The Chinese Garden), a perfect replica of one from the Ming dynasty designed to celebrate the friendship between the two cities. Lakes, rocks and plants strive for a harmonious blend of yin and yang: small and large, soft and hard, light and dark, flowing and immovable. Look for the seven pavilions, central reflecting pool, rockery and collection of miniature trees known as "penjings" (displayed in a greenhouse in winter). The Japanese Garden and Pavilion are exquisite, as is the summer collection of bonsai trees.

THE BASICS

espacepourlavie.ca

✚ F1

✉ 4101 rue Sherbrooke Est

☎ 514/ 872-1400

🕑 Late Jun–Sep daily 9–6; Sep–Oct daily 9–9; Nov–late Jun daily 9–5

🍴 Café

Ⓠ Viau, Pie-IX

🚌 185

♿ Very good

💲 Expensive. Parking fee

❓ Free shuttle bus from Le Biodôme, Parc Olympique and Viau Métro

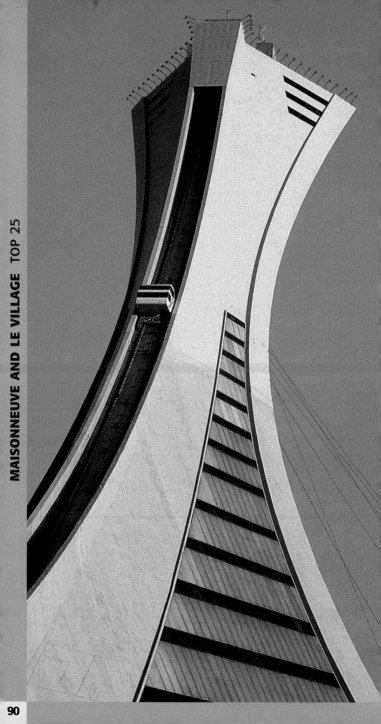

The Montréal Tower (opposite) and a view from the top (right); Olympic Stadium (left)

Parc Olympique

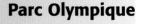

While the Stade Olympique left a deep financial hole that still plagues the city 40 years later, it has become part of Montréal's modern architectural heritage.

Soaring costs When Mayor Jean Drapeau persuaded Montréalers to host the Olympic Games in 1976, he promised that the event wouldn't cost them a cent. French architect Roger Taillibert set to work, believing money was no object. Both were wrong. The stadium and its tower cost $1.2 (US) billion, but it has never been a success as a sports venue, abandoned by the local football team, and the Expos, Montréal's major-league baseball team, after the franchise moved. The space makes its money on trade shows, occasional sports games and huge concerts. But it's impressively bright and airy, and worth seeing.

Leaning tower It is not so much the stadium that pulls in visitors as the park's famous inclined tower (Tour de Montréal), built to support the stadium's retractable roof (which itself is set to be renewed by 2023). Since it opened in 1989, more than 5 million people have ascended to the observation platform. The 175m (575ft) ascent via an external cable car is stomach churning, but you are rewarded with a view that on a clear day stretches for 80km (50 miles). Galleries in the tower's lower levels contain displays about the park's history, and the Tourist Hall at the tower's base has information, tickets and exhibits.

THE BASICS

parcolympique.qc.ca

🔲 G2

✉ 4141 avenue Pierre-de-Coubertin

☎ 514/252-4141 or 877/997-0919

🕐 Mid-Jun to early Sep daily 9–7; early Sep to mid-Jun Tue–Sun 9–6, Mon 1–5. Closed early Jan to mid-Feb

🍴 Café (summer only)

🚇 Viau or Pie-IX (free shuttle from Viau mid-May to late Oct 11–5)

🚌 185

♿ Very good

💰 Tower: expensive. Tours: moderate

❓ Souvenir shop

TIPS

● Use the sports center's fitness classes, swimming pool and badminton courts.
● The *Since 1976* exhibition ($18.50 adult, $9.25 child) is a guided tour of the park and sports centre.
● Ride up the tower to the observation deck (Tue–Sun 9-5, $23.25 adult, $11.50 child).

More to See

CHÂTEAU DUFRESNE

chateaudufresne.qc.ca

Little in the symmetrical Beaux-Arts facade of this building suggests that it is two buildings, built between 1915 and 1918 for brothers Marius and Oscar Dufresne. Marius, the architect, lived in the west wing and his brother in the east wing. When the Dufresne families moved on, the house became a boys' school in the 1950s under the guardianship of priests, who covered many of the friezes and murals. Many have been rediscovered, along with much of the original interiors, offering a vivid insight into the lives of Montréal's Francophone elite at the beginning of the 20th century. It is the sumptuous interiors that prove most compelling, with marble staircases, gold-damask hangings, mahogany-covered walls, stained-glass windows and beautiful coffered ceilings.

➕ F2 ✉ 2929 avenue Jeanne-d'Arc ☎ 514/259-9201 ⏰ Wed–Sun 9.30–5 🚇 Pie-IX 🚹 Good 🎟 Moderate

ÉCOMUSÉE DU FIER MONDE

ecomusee.qc.ca

Photographs and period objects illustrate the Industrial Revolution and its impact on Montréal and its people.

➕ E8 ✉ 2050 rue Amherst ☎ 514/528-8444 ⏰ Wed 11–8, Thu–Fri 9.30–4, Sat–Sun 10.30–5 🚇 Berri-UQAM 🚌 14, 15, 125 🚹 Good 🎟 Moderate

MAISONNEUVE

Maisonneuve was a model city, created by French-speaking citizens who preferred to be separated from the then predominantly Anglo-Saxon city of Montréal. For 35 years from 1883 it was a self-contained city, as the ruling elite commissioned wide boulevards and fine public buildings, many designed by Marius Dufresne. Seek out the Fire Station (4300 rue Notre-Dame Est), which owes an architectural debt to Frank Lloyd Wright, the Beaux-Arts Marché Maisonneuve (▷ below) and the former public baths opposite. Also eye-catching

A Beaux-Arts delight, Château Dufresne is just as sumptuous inside

are the Théatre Denise Pelletier, near the junction of rue Morgan and rue Sainte-Catherine Est, and the Église Très-Saint-Nom-de-Jésus.

➕ H2 🚇 Pie-XI, Joliette, Viau

MARCHÉ MAISONNEUVE

marchespublics-mtl.com

The original Marché Maisonneuve, a magnificent 1912 Beaux Arts building, is now a cultural center, but farmers still sell their produce in the modern building next door.

➕ H2 ✉ 4445 rue Ontario Est
☎ 514/937-7754 ⏰ Mon–Wed, Sat 7–6, Thu–Fri 7am–8pm, Sun 7–5 🚇 Pie-XI, Viau

PARC MAISONNEUVE

Parc Maisonneuve's slopes and frozen lakes provide a great spot for tobogganing, cross-country skiing and skating in winter. In summer the park is ideal for picnics, walking, cycling, and you can even play golf.

➕ E1 ✉ 4601 rue Sherbrooke Est and boulevard Pie-XI ☎ 514/872-6555 ⏰ Daily 6am–9pm 🚇 Viau, Pie-IX ♿ Good 💲 Park free. Golf course/parking moderate

RIO TINTO ALCAN PLANETARIUM

espacepourlavie.ca/en/planetarium

Montréal's state-of-the-art planetarium forms part of the Olympic Park and Biodôme-Insectarium-Jardin Botanique ensemble. Settle back on reclining chairs or beanbags to enjoy an immersive astronomical experience that combines both art and science. Note that the shows play more often in French than in English so check the times first.

➕ G1 ✉ 4801 avenue Pierre-De-Coubertin
☎ 514/868-3000 or 514/872-4530 ⏰ Tue–Wed 9–5, Thu–Sat 9–8, Sun 9–5 🚇 Viau
🚌 34, 125, 132 💲 Expensive

LE VILLAGE

A few blocks from the Quartier Latin, the Village is the heart of Montréal's vibrant LGBTQ community. It's especially lively during the *Divers Cité* festival in August and Black & Blue festival in October.

➕ F8 ✉ rue Sainte-Catherine, roughly from St-Hubert to De Lorimier 🚇 Beaudry or Papineau

Cycling through Maisonneuve Park on a bicycle made for two

Shopping

A L'ANTIQUITÉ CURIOSITÉ

An army of chairs, lamps, and other furnishings and retro accessories dating from the 1930s to the 1980s greet you at this treasure-trove, but it's the beautifully restored Mad Men-era teak pieces that steal the show. It's known for its helpful service, with knowledgable staff on hand to happily answer questions, whether you're a seasoned collector or a novice browser hoping for a bargain.

🔒 F9 ✉ 1769 rue Amherst ☎ 514/525-8772 🕐 Mon–Fri 11–6, Sat–Sun 11–5 🚇 Berri-UQAM

BOUTIQUE SPOUTNIK

boutiquespoutnik.com

For a unique souvenir, Spoutnik is a veritable treasure trove of late-20th century curiosities, and collectors will fall in love with its vintage lamps, sleek Danish *fauteuils* and coffee tables, and amusing mod and space-aged pieces. Owner Sylvie Rochon is also very good with her hands and will lovingly repurpose items such as embroidered portraits of dogs into charming cushion covers.

🔒 D9 ✉ 2120 rue Amherst ☎ 514/525-8478 🕐 Tue–Sat 12–5 🚇 Sherbrooke

Where to Eat

PRICES	
Prices are approximate, based on a 3-course meal for one person.	
$$$	over $45
$$	$25–$45
$	under $25

AGRIKOL ($$)

agrikol.ca

Co-owned by Win Butler and wife Régine Chassagne of famed Montréal indie rock band Arcade Fire, whose parents emigrated here from Haiti, Agrikol is a lively, whimsically decorated venture in Le Village. It serves up Creole classics like *conch ceviche*, *maïs moulu* (polenta) *accras* (malanga-root fritters) with *pikliz* (a spicy condiment), amid bottles of Barbancourt rum and the seductive rhythms of *kompa* music. Agrikol also boasts a leafy, lantern-lit rear terrace that oozes island charm.

🔒 F9 ✉ 1844 rue Amherst ☎ 514/903-6575 🕐 Daily 6pm–midnight 🚇 Berri-UQAM or Beaudry

LE MOUSSO ($$$)

Opened in 2015, this restaurant is considered one of the best newer restos in the city. It has a minimalist decor and no website or wine list (cocktails and wines are served by the glass and chosen specifically to pair with each dish). Chef Antonin Mousseau-Rivard's beautifully presented dishes are as much works of art as they are imaginative flavour-and-texture combinations for the taste buds.

🔒 F8 ✉ 1023 rue Ontario Est ☎ 438/384-7410 🕐 Wed–Sun dinner 🚇 Berri-UQAM

At the fringes of Montréal's down-town core, and at the heart of the Saint Lawrence River, are two islands and a variety of sights that are well worth making a special journey to visit.

Farther Afield and the Islands

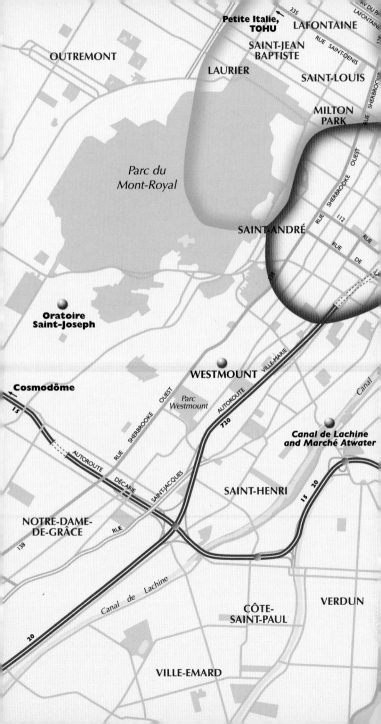

Petite Italie, TOHU
335
LAFONTAINE
LAFONTAINE

OUTREMONT

SAINT-JEAN BAPTISTE

RUE SAINT-DENIS

LAURIER

SAINT-LOUIS

RUE SHERBROOKE

MILTON PARK

Parc du Mont-Royal

RUE SHERBROOKE OUEST

112

SAINT-ANDRÉ

RUE

RUE DE L

138

●
Oratoire Saint-Joseph

VILLE-MARIE

●
WESTMOUNT

←
Cosmodôme
15

Parc Westmount

RUE SHERBROOKE OUEST

AUTOROUTE

720

Canal

●
Canal de Lachine and Marché Atwater

AUTOROUTE DÉCARIE

SAINT-JACQUES

SAINT-HENRI

15 20

NOTRE-DAME-DE-GRÂCE

RUE

138

Canal de Lachine

CÔTE-SAINT-PAUL

VERDUN

20

VILLE-EMARD

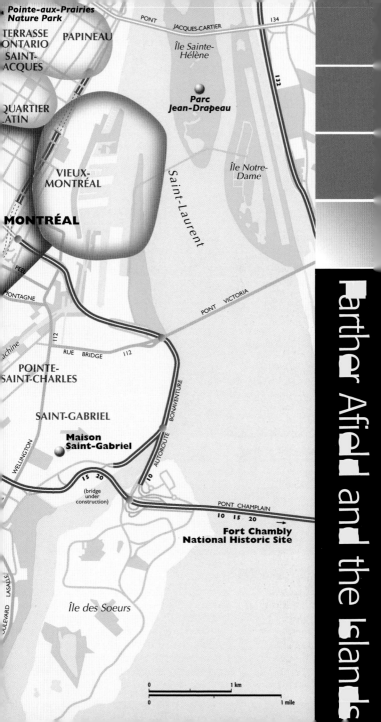

Pointe-aux-Prairies
Nature Park

PONT JACQUES-CARTIER

134

TERRASSE
ONTARIO

PAPINEAU

132

SAINT-
ACQUES

Île Sainte-
Hélène

QUARTIER
ATIN

Parc
Jean-Drapeau

VIEUX-
MONTRÉAL

Île Notre-
Dame

Saint-Laurent

MONTRÉAL

PEEL

MONTAGNE

PONT VICTORIA

achine

112

RUE BRIDGE   112

POINTE-
SAINT-CHARLES

SAINT-GABRIEL

BONAVENTURE

WELLINGTON

Maison
Saint-Gabriel

AUTOROUTE

15 20

10

(bridge
under
construction)

PONT CHAMPLAIN

10   15   20

**Fort Chambly
National Historic Site**

LASALLE

OULEVARD

Île des Soeurs

0   1 km

0   1 mile

Canal de Lachine and Marché Atwater

HIGHLIGHTS

● Guided tours of the canal
● Boating on the canal
● Cycling the canalside path
● Sampling the fare at the Atwater Market

TIP

● There are two best times to visit Marché Atwater: weekday mornings for hassle-free shopping; after-work hours and Saturdays for bustling people-watching.

The former industrial canal offers historic sites, waterside walks and boating. The nearby Marché Atwater is full of enticing aromas and colorful food displays.

From industry to leisure When it opened in 1825, the Canal de Lachine bypassed the Lachine Rapids to provide a lifeline between the industries of Lachine and their worldwide trading partners. Later industrial decline, coupled with the opening of the Saint Lawrence Seaway, led to the canal becoming neglected, and it closed in 1970. Its historic importance was never forgotten, though, and a massive restoration project led to its reopening in 2002 as a National Historic Site of Canada. Locks were restored, the Peel basin was dredged, bridges were renovated and a Visitor Service Centre

Clockwise from left: on a bicycle path at Lachine Canal; Marché Atwater sells a wide range of fresh foods; a nursery at Marché Atwater catches the attention of a cyclist; patisserie on sale at the market; Lachine National Historic Site

built. Now pleasure craft and cruise boats dot the water in summer, and its 14.5km (9 miles) between the Old Port and Lac St.-Louis in Lachine are lined by pedestrian and cycle paths and picnic places. There is an interesting exhibition on the history of the fur trade.

Atwater You can't miss the Marché Atwater, a monumental art deco building with a tall clock tower, particularly during summer when the stands spill outside. With two floors undercover, it has a magnificent array of quality foods, including deli goods, fish and sushi, gourmet foods, cheese specialists, butchers, bakers, a beer store, and beautifully displayed fresh fruit, vegetables and flowers. If you want to shop for the finest local and organic produce, or hard-to-find imported specialties, this is your place.

THE BASICS

Lachine Canal National Historic Site
pc.gc.ca/lhn-nhs/qc/canal-lachine
➕ F14/C17
✉ From Vieux-Port to Lachine
☎ 514/283-6054
🕐 Daily sunrise–11pm. Fur Trade Museum: mid-Jun to Sep 1 daily 10–5
🚇 Lionel-Groulx, Charlevoix
🚌 57, 61, 78, 107, 195
💰 Canal: free; parking inexpensive
❓ Guided tours

Atwater Market
marchespublics-mtl.com
➕ D16
✉ 138 avenue Atwater
☎ 514/937-7754
🕐 Mon–Wed 7–6, Thu 7–7, Fri 7am–8pm, Sat–Sun 7–5
🚇 Lionel-Groulx
🚌 78, 195

Petite Italie

Trattorias, ristorantes and caffès; gelati, espresso and pasta; a park and street named after Dante; and a fine Romanesque church—there's little doubt that this is Montréal's Italian quarter.

From the old country There have been two main waves of Italian immigration into Montréal—the first at the end of the 19th century, and again after World War II, and, though the area is now home to a more eclectic mix, it is still the Italian culture that predominates.

Cultural treasures Thanks to its distance from downtown, the character of Little Italy has remained relatively intact. Shopping is a major attraction. Explore its section of boulevard Saint-Laurent and rue Dante, which form the

Shop for local ingredients and eat at one of the district's trattorias

commercial hub for Italian fashion and footwear designs, restaurants and cafés; or head for the Marché Jean-Talon for fresh ingredients and gourmet foods. Be sure to allow time to visit the splendid Madonna della Difesa Church on avenue Henri-Julien, a fine Romanesque building with a Carrara marble altar and remarkable frescoes by Guido Nincheri (1885–1973). Dante Park, next to the church, is a great place for relaxing and people-watching, and the Casa d'Italia is the local community center.

Festival time Each August the Semaine Italienne (Italian Week; italianweek.ca) celebrates Montréal's Italian community with music, dance, theater and, of course, food and drink. The rest of the time, there's nothing better than a spot of window-shopping.

THE BASICS

➕ See map ▷ 96
✉ Between rues Saint-Zotique, Drolet, Jean-Talon and avenue du Parc
🚇 Jean-Talon
🚌 30, 55
Marché Jean-Talon
marchespublics-mtl.com
✉ 7070 rue Henri-Julien
☎ 514/937-7754
🕐 Mon–Wed 7–6, Thu–Fri 7am–8pm, Sat 7–6, Sun 7–5
🚇 Jean-Talon

Parc Jean-Drapeau

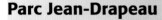

HIGHLIGHTS

● La Biosphère
● La Ronde amusement park
● Musée Stewart
● Public art
● The beach

TIPS

● You can save waiting time for rides at La Ronde with the Flash Pass reservation system.
● The dress code at the casino is not too strict (except for Nuances restaurant), but is worth checking out before a visit. The minimum age is 18.

Two islands in the Saint Lawrence River provide a vast playground close to downtown, offering theme-park rides, motor racing, concerts, gambling, a historic site and an environmental museum.

La Biosphère When Expo '67 opened, the US Pavilion was then the world's largest geodesic dome. It went on to become the world's largest aviary, but after fire destroyed its acrylic skin in 1976 the metal skeleton was all that survived. Today this great transparent golf ball encloses a fascinating environmental museum, run by the government agency Environment Canada. In addition to the exhibits and multimedia activities, there are guided tours to explain the building's wind turbine and geothermal power systems and its wastewater treatment wetlands.

Clockwise from top left: Formula 1 Grand Prix race at the Gilles-Villeneuve circuit; La Biosphère; entrance to La Ronde amusement park; the casino; Alexander Calder's sculpture, Man, *on Île Sainte-Hélène; La Ronde*

Île Notre-Dame When the Métro system was being excavated in the 1960s, they needed somewhere to deposit all the waste, and the then mayor, Jean Drapeau, decided to create an island to host the upcoming world fair. Former pavilions from the fair house a casino, the Gilles-Villeneuve motor-racing circuit hosts the Canadian Grand Prix, an artificial lakeside beach is a huge attraction, and there's a vast floral park, laced with canals and waterways.

Île Saint-Hélène Île Saint-Hélène was linked to the city when the Jacques Cartier bridge was built in 1930, then doubled in size (more Métro rubble) for Expo '67. Now it is known for the La Ronde amusement park, open-air concerts, summer fireworks competitions and the Musée Stewart history museum.

THE BASICS

parcjeandrapeau.com

⊞ J6–11

✉ Société du parc Jean-Drapeau, 1 circuit Gilles-Villeneuve

☎ 514/872- 6120 🕓 Île Ste-Hélène 6am–10pm, Île Notre-Dame 6am–midnight 🍴 Restaurants and snack bars on both islands

🚇 Jean-Drapeau

🚌 167 (year-round), 169 (seasonal) 🚢 Jacques-Cartier Pier 🖐 Free; beach moderate; parking inexpensive

La Biosphère

biosphere.ec.gc.ca

✉ 160 Chemin Tour-de-l'Isle, Île Sainte-Hélène

☎ 514/283-5000

🕓 Jun– Sep daily 10–5; Oct–May Wed–Sun 10–5

🖐 Moderate

La Ronde

laronde.com

✉ 22 Chemin Macdonald, Île Sainte-Hélène

☎ 514/397-2000

🕓 Mid-May to early Sep daily from 10am; Sep daily from noon; Oct Sat–Sun from noon. Closing varies seasonally 🖐 Expensive

Musée Stewart

stewart-museum.org

✉ Île Sainte-Hélène

☎ 514/861-6701 Wed–Sun 11–5 🖐 Moderate

Casino de Montréal

casinosduquebec.com

✉ Île Notre-Dame

☎ 514/392-2746

🕓 Daily 24 hours

🚇 Jean-Drapeau 🚌 167

More to See

COSMODÔME

cosmodome.org

The adventure of space exploration is the focus here. Exhibits include replicas of rockets and space ships, films, games and demonstrations.

See map ▷ 96 2150 autoroute de Laurentides, Laval 450/978-3600 or 800/565-2267 Late Jun to mid-Sep daily 9–5; mid-Sep to late Jun daily 10–5 Montmorency, then bus 61 Expensive

FORT CHAMBLY NATIONAL HISTORIC SITE

pc.gc.ca

Standing beside the Richelieu River, close to where it tumbles over the Chambly rapids, this great square bastion was built by the French in the early 18th century to replace a wooden fort. The British took it over, after their conquest of "New France," and stood guard here as American forces threatened, first during their Revolutionary War and then in the war of 1812. The fort survived and was restored in the 1980s. Today, it houses exhibitions about the life of the early French settlers. Guides are on hand to discuss the history of the fort. There are also colorful special events, with costumed re-enactments.

See map ▷ 97 2 rue de Richelieu, Chambly 450/658-1585 or 888/773-8888 Mid-May to late Jun and early Sep to late Oct Wed–Sun 10–5; late Jun to Aug daily 10–6 Chambly-Richelieu-Carignan from downtown Moderate

MAISON SAINT-GABRIEL

maisonsaint-gabriel.qc.ca

St. Marguerite Bourgeoys ran a farm and school from this 17th-century house among Pointe-Saint-Charles tenements. In addition to special exhibitions, the house has some 15,000 objects from the 17th century onward, including furniture, art and craft works, tools and artifacts, clothing, silverware and documents.

F16 2146 place Dublin 514/935-8136 Late Jun to early Sep Tue–Sun 11–6; mid-Apr to late Jun, early Sep to mid-Dec Tue–Sun 1–5 Charlevoix 57, 61 Good Moderate

Maison Saint-Gabriel, dating back to 1668, is now a heritage museum

POINTE-AUX-PRAIRIES NATURE PARK

ville.montreal.qc.ca

This park sits at the northeastern tip of Montréal island, where the Saint Lawrence river meets the Rivière des Prairies, and covers 261ha (645 acres) of forest, pastures and marshland. Special pathways have been set out for birding, and activities range from cycling and rollerblading in summer to cross-country skiing and tobogganing in winter.

🦰 See map ▷ 97 ✉ 14905 rue Sherbrooke Est ☎ 514/280-6691 ⏰ Park: daily dawn–dusk; Heritage Centre: late Apr to late Oct daily 9.30–4.30; Nature Interpretation Centre: late Apr to mid-Sep Wed–Mon 9.30–4.30 🚇 Honoré-Meaugrand, then bus 186 🍴 Snack bar 🎫 Free; parking inexpensive

TOHU

tohu.ca

This round building out in the Complexe Environnemental de Saint-Michel is a center for the circus arts and incorporates an exciting performance space and exhibitions.

🦰 See map ▷ 96 ✉ 2345 rue Jarry Est ☎ 888/376-8648 ⏰ Box office daily noon–5 🚇 Jarry, then bus 193 east; Iberville, then bus 94 north 🚌 57, 61 🦽 Very good

WESTMOUNT

westmount.org

On the western slopes of Mont-Royal, Westmount mixes fine English-style mansions, parks, specialty shopping and modern architecture, of which Westmount Square—a black metal and tinted-glass building by van der Rohe—is the showpiece. In Parc Westmount, older buildings are the 1899 Victoria Hall, a community center, and the 1927 Conservatory, which produces plants for the city and has a totem pole from British Columbia.

🦰 B15 🚇 Vendôme, Atwater 🚌 24, 37, 63, 66, 90, 104, 124, 138

Victoria Hall Gallery and Conservatory

✉ 4626 rue Sherbrooke Ouest ☎ 514/989-5353 ⏰ Conservatory: Mon–Fri 10–2.30, Sat–Sun 10–4.45 🎫 Free

Westmount Square, a striking building by Mies van der Rohe

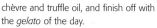

Where to Eat

PRICES	
Prices are approximate, based on a 3-course meal for one person.	
$$$	over $45
$$	$25–$45
$	under $25

JOE BEEF ($$)

joebeef.com

Joe Beef is named for a tavern-keeper who was the hero of this formerly blue-collar neighborhood. The atmosphere is old-time and the beef is big-time.

🚩 D15 ✉ 2491 rue Notre-Dame Ouest ☎ 514/935-6504 🕐 Tue–Sat 6pm–10.30pm 🚇 Lionel-Groulx

LIVERPOOL HOUSE ($$)

joebeef.com

The oyster bar and seafood are the draw at this popular St.-Henri eatery with a seaside cottage feel. Don't be surprised to run into Prime Minister Justin Trudeau; he's a regular and dined here with Obama in June 2017.

🚩 D15 ✉ 2501 rue Notre-Dame Ouest ☎ 514/313-6049 🕐 Tue–Sat from 5pm 🚇 Lionel-Groulx

PASTICCERIA ALATI-CASERTA ($)

alaticaserta.com

There's no place to sit, but just join the people on the street outside, all munching on the best *cannoli* (a sweet pastry) in town. Everything, from the dough to the frosting, is done in-house.

🚩 Off map ✉ 277 rue Dante ☎ 514/271-3013 🕐 Mon 10–5, Tue–Wed 8–6, Thu 8–7, Fri 8–7.30, Sat 8–5.30, Sun 9–5 🚇 Jean-Talon

PIZZERIA GEPPETTO ($$)

geppettopizza.com

This little Italian spot serves pizzas beyond the usual—try mushroom with chèvre and truffle oil, and finish off with the *gelato* of the day.

🚩 D15 ✉ 2504 rue Notre-Dame Ouest ☎ 514/903-3737 🕐 Mon–Wed 11.30–10, Thu–Fri 11.30am–midnight, Sat 5pm–midnight, Sun 5pm–10pm 🚇 Lionel-Groulx

PIZZERIA NAPOLETANA ($$)

napoletana.com

Bring your own wine (big carafes of cold water are free) to this crowded, friendly spot, Montréal's first pizzeria. Famed for thin-crust pizza and pasta dishes, it offers 41 different types of pizza and 34 pasta options.

🚩 Off map ✉ 189 rue Dante ☎ 514/276-8226 🕐 Mon–Thu 11–11, Fri–Sat 11am–midnight, Sun noon–11 🚇 De Castelneau

PREMIÈRE MOISSON ($)

premieremoisson.com

A branch of this *charcuterie* and bakery chain is located at the canal end of the Atwater Market. Come here for flaky croissants and *café au lait* in a bowl, for *cretons* (a pork spread) on a baguette, or just to admire a beautiful cake. Other branches are at the Jean-Talon Market and 22 other outlets around the city.

🚩 D16 ✉ Atwater Market, 138 avenue Atwater ☎ 514/932-0328 🕐 Mon–Wed 7–6, Thu 7–7, Fri 7am–8pm, Sat–Sun 7–5 🚇 Lionel-Groulx

QUOI DE N'OEUFS ($)

restocafequoidenoeuf.ca

Enjoy great eggs Benedict and other creative egg dishes for brunch while shopping at Atwater Market. It's also worth trying for its crêpes and French toast. There may be a line, but it's worth joining as it moves fast.

🚩 D15 ✉ 2745 rue Notre-Dame Ouest ☎ 514/931-3999 🕐 Mon–Sat 7am–2.45pm, Sun 8am–2.45pm 🚇 Lionel-Groulx

Whether you like to stay in the thick of it or opt for some peace and quiet, or prefer large chain hotels rather than a more intimate establishment, Montréal can satisfy all tastes.

Where to Stay

Introduction

Montréal has a wide range of high-quality accommodations, from boutique hotels in the old port area to glittering luxury places in the downtown and Mont-Royal districts.

Where to Stay

The most charming area to stay is Vieux-Montréal, where around a dozen intimate and interesting hotels in the mid- and luxury ranges offer accommodations close to the city's main historic sights. If you prefer to be nearer to the best shopping, or want a larger, international or chain hotel, then the best bet is downtown, which is still convenient for sightseeing. Budget hotels are relatively thin on the ground, except in the Quartier Latin and around, though here the location, while good for nightlife and dining options, is far less appealing. Places near the bus station, in particular, are best avoided.

Best to Book

Although Montreál has plenty of accommodations, with more hotels opening every year, the city's increasing popularity with visitors means that it can still be difficult to secure a place to stay in high season and other busy times. Always book well ahead if you plan to visit from May to September, in the busy shopping weeks before Christmas, or during popular events. Try contacting the visitor center for last-minute and other options. Or consider staying in one of the city's many bed-and-breakfasts, though these can be some way from the city hub.

SAVING MONEY

Smaller hotels often have a variety of rooms at different prices, so don't assume the first room you are offered is the cheapest. Hotels that cater predominantly to business people often offer discounted weekend rates. Many hotels also offer discounted rates online and for longer stays. Tourisme Montréal has a year-round Sweet Deals promotion offering discounted hotel rooms (tourisme-montreal.org/offers). Always ask what is included in a rate, especially regarding breakfasts.

Budget Hotels

ANNE MA SOEUR ANNE

annemasoeuranne.com

A good-value hotel in the upscale Plateau district that has excellent in-room facilities, including high-speed WiFi, voicemail, microwave, toaster-oven and coffee-maker. Continental breakfast is included.

➕ D8 ✉ 4119 rue Saint-Denis ☎ 514/281-3187 or 877/281-3187 🚇 Mont-Royal, Sherbrooke

AUBERGE YWCA

aubergeywca.com

Situated on the 6th floor of the YWCA, the Auberge provides simple and convenient accommodations downtown, near the Bell Centre. The 32 rooms offer single, double or triple occupancy, with shared bathrooms and showers.

➕ D12 ✉ 1355 boulevard René-Lévesque Ouest ☎ 514/866-9942 🚇 Lucien L'Allier

BIENVENUE B&B

bienvenuebb.com

This cozy bed-and-breakfast is on a pleasant residential street of old stone houses, close to the buzzing rue Saint-Denis and boulevard Saint-Laurent. The 12 rooms are individually styled and some have private bathrooms.

➕ D9 ✉ 3950 avenue Laval ☎ 514/844-5897 or 800/227-5897 🚇 Sherbrooke

HÔTEL AMBROSE

hotelambrose.ca

Rooms in this beautiful 19th-century greystone in the Golden Mile are simply decorated in snow whites and dove greys, with some of the original architectural details still intact. There's a café in the lobby which serves excellent breakfasts, including avocado toast.

➕ C11 ✉ 3422 rue Stanley ☎ 514/288-6922 🚇 Peel

HÔTEL LE ROBERVAL

leroberval.com

Centrally located no-frills hotel with 76 rooms and small apartments with kitchenettes. Serves continental breakfast. Some rooms have balconies, wood floors and exposed brick walls.

➕ F9 ✉ 505 boulevard René-Lévesque Est ☎ 514/552-2992 🚇 Champ-de-Mars, Berri-UQAM

MCGILL UNIVERSITY

mcgill.ca/accommodations/summer

During the summer recess (mid-May to Aug), visitors can rent student lodgings at McGill University—more than 1,000 rooms. While some of these accommodations are more like modern highrise hotels, with a seasonal on-site café and en-suite bathroom, most are inexpensive and more like traditional student dormitories in a pleasant campus setting and include the use of the university gym, pool and other facilities—some with access to kitchenettes.

➕ D11 ✉ 3935 rue University ☎ 514/398-5200 or 3471 (new Residence Hall) 🚇 McGill

BED-AND-BREAKFAST

B&B options can be booked through tourist offices and at tourisme-montreal.org, the city's official tourism site, which has numerous and regularly updated deals across all price ranges, along with a useful neighborhood search option. Good websites for bed-and-breakfast in Montréal include bedandbreakfast.com and canadianbandbguide.ca.

Mid-Range Hotels

PRICES
Expect to pay between $150 and $280 for a mid-range hotel

AUBERGE BONAPARTE
bonaparte.com
This delightful 31-room inn, in the heart of Vieux-Montréal, has views of the gardens of the Basilique Notre-Dame, which are right next door.
✚ F11 ✉ 447 rue Saint-François-Xavier ☎ 514/844-1448 🚇 Place d'Armes

AUBERGE LES BONS MATINS
bonsmatins.com
Cozy century-old B&B spread across a row of Victorian houses in a leafy downtown cul-de-sac just a seven-minute walk to the Bell Centre. Its colorful rooms have some stunning features and wonderful breakfasts are served.
✚ D13 ✉ 1401 avenue Argyle ☎ 514/931-9167 or 800/588-5280 🚇 Lucien L'Allier

AUBERGE DE LA FONTAINE
aubergelejardindantoine.com
With just 18 rooms and three suites, this intimate hotel faces Parc Lafontaine in the trendy Plateau Mont-Royal district. It is a welcoming little inn with vivid but appealing decorations and a good breakfast included in the room rate.
✚ D7 ✉ 1301 rue Rachel Est ☎ 514/597-0166 or 800/597-0597 🚇 Mont-Royal

AUBERGE LE JARDIN D'ANTOINE
aubergejardinantoine.com
Reproduction antiques lend a charming period feel to this 25-room hotel, which sits at the heart of the rue Saint-Denis and Quartier Latin nightlife and entertainment district.
✚ E9 ✉ 2024 rue Saint-Denis ☎ 514/843-4506 or 800/361-4506 🚇 Berri-UQAM

AUBERGE DE LA PLACE ROYALE
aubergedelaplaceroyale.com
A B&B in a fine 19th-century Vieux-Port building, with nine moderate rooms and three suites. Rooms have parquet flooring and are filled with reproductions of antiques, with views of the waterfront from the most expensive rooms. The other rooms look onto a back street.
✚ G11 ✉ 115 rue de la Commune Ouest ☎ 514/287-0522 🚇 Place d'Armes

CHÂTEAU VERSAILLES
chateauversaillesmontreal.com
An elegant hotel with Old World charm housed in four former townhouses in the Golden Square Mile, one of which was owned by the 14th Lieutenant-Governor of Quebec. The former residences-turned-hotel rooms still retain some of the original mouldings, ceiling friezes, and ornate Dutch fireplaces, as well as an art deco lamp.
✚ C13 ✉ 1659 rue Sherbrooke Ouest ☎ 514/933-3611 or 888/933-8111 🚇 Guy-Concordia

HÔTEL ARMOR MANOIR SHERBROOKE
armormanoir.com
Converted Victorian greystone with 22 rooms with hardwood floors. Many original features such as a marble fireplace and ornately carved mahogany arches in common areas are still intact.
✚ E9 ✉ 157 rue Sherbrooke Est ☎ 514/845-0915 or 800/203-5485 🚇 Sherbrooke

HÔTEL DE L'INSTITUT
ithq.qc.ca
Top civil servants love this 42-room hotel on the top floors of Québec's best hotel training school, right in the Quartier Latin.

✚ E9 ✉ 3535 rue Saint-Denis ☎ 514/282-5120 or 855/229-8189 🚇 Sherbrooke

HÔTEL LORD BERRI

lordberri.com

Good modern hotel with 154 rooms near the Université du Québec à Montréal and rue Saint-Denis.
✚ F19 ✉ 1199 rue Berri ☎ 514/845-9236 or 888/363-0363 🚇 Berri-UQAM

HÔTEL WILLIAM GRAY

hotelwilliamgray.com

Opened in 2016, Hôtel William Gray juxtaposes old and new with its two 18th-century Old Montréal buildings topped by a new eight-story glass tower. The lobby is alluring, with its stairway, low-slung furniture and gas fireplace. The rooms, with white oak floors, white walls and gauzy curtains feel fresh and airy. Restaurant Maggie Oakes and the rooftop terrace, with its excellent views of the Old Port, are also big draws.
✚ F10 ✉ 412 rue St-Vincent ☎ 514/656-5600 🚇 Place d'Armes

LOEWS HÔTEL VOGUE

loewshotels.com

The 142 rooms and suites of this fashionable downtown hotel with its greenhouse-style lobby and French bistro all have whirlpool baths.
✚ D12 ✉ 1425 rue de la Montagne ☎ 514/285-5555 or 866/727-1607 🚇 Peel, Guy-Concordia

LE PETIT HÔTEL

petithotelmontreal.com

This stylish boutique hotel in an old greystone, close to Vieux Montréal and the waterfront, features stone walls, high ceilings and windows, and sleek modern furniture. Breakfast and local telephone calls are included.

✚ F11 ✉ 168 rue Saint-Paul Ouest ☎ 514/940-0360 or 877/530-0360 🚇 Place d'Armes

LE SAINT-SULPICE

lesaintsulpice.com

A good location—by the Basilique Notre-Dame—is the draw of this 108-room hotel, in a modern building designed to blend with its period surroundings.
✚ F11 ✉ 414 rue Saint-Sulpice ☎ 514/288-1000 or 877/785-7423 🚇 Place d'Armes

SIR MONTCALM

sirmontcalm.com

Located in Le Village, this chic B&B is gay-owned and operated but is straight-friendly too. The contemporary decor is stunning and the price even includes a four-course breakfast.
✚ F9 ✉ 1453 Montcalm ☎ 514/522-7747 🚇 Beaudry

SOFITEL MONTRÉAL

sofitel.com

This modern skyscraper hotel has 241 bright, spacious rooms with stylish interiors and floor-to-ceiling windows.
✚ D12 ✉ 1155 rue Sherbrooke Ouest ☎ 514/285-9000 or 877/285-9001 🚇 Peel

HIDDEN COSTS

To avoid any nasty shocks on checking out of your hotel, it is worth knowing the various taxes and other hidden charges that will appear on Montréal bills. Some hotels will include these charges in the published room rate: Most will not. The additions include the country-wide Goods and Services Tax (GST) at 5 percent and a provincial sales tax of 7.5 percent. There is also a city tax of 5 percent. Be aware that hotels will also often charge high rates for any direct-dial calls made from your room.

Luxury Hotels

FAIRMONT LE REINE ELIZABETH

fairmont.com

This long-established, 1,000-plus room hotel just underwent a $140-million renovation. It is where John Lennon and Yoko Ono staged their famous "bed-in for peace" in 1969, in suite no. 1742. It has excellent modern rooms and service, especially on the "Gold Floor."

➕ E12 ✉ 900 boulevard René-Lévesque Ouest ☎ 514/861-3511 or 866/540-4483 🚇 Bonaventure

HÔTEL NELLIGAN

hotelnelligan.com

A beautiful, romantic hotel in an 1850s building, with 35 rooms and 28 suites. The characterful rooms feature exposed brick and other original features, while the service is exemplary.

➕ F11 ✉ 106 rue Saint-Paul Ouest ☎ 514/788-2040 or 877/788-2040 🚇 Place d'Armes

HÔTEL LE ST-JAMES

hotellestjames.com

Built in 1870, this grand building, which once housed a bank, is supremely luxurious in the classic style of its era, with an elegant sweeping staircase leading from a lofty entrance hall. The rooms and suites are spacious.

➕ F11 ✉ 355 rue St-Jacques ☎ 514/841-3111 or 866/841-3111 🚇 Square-Victoria, Place d'Armes

LE MOUNT STEPHEN

lemountstephen.com

This lavish heritage hotel opened in May 2017. With its ornate, carved woodwork, stained-glass windows, crystal chandeliers and period furniture, Bar George is a popular spot. By contrast, the 90 ultra-modern and luxurious rooms and suites have Toto toilets, chromotherapy rainforest showerheads and heated floors. They're in the purpose-built 11-story tower next door—accessible by a tunnel.

➕ C12 ✉ 1440 rue Drummond ☎ 514/313-1000 or 844/838-8655 🚇 Peel

SAINT PAUL HÔTEL

hotelstpaul.com

At Montréal's first design hotel you can choose between airy, white rooms with large windows and the darker, more dramatic 10th-floor suite with charcoal walls. Look out for the giant alabaster fireplace, built of backlit blocks of "ice," in the chic, minimalist lobby.

➕ F12 ✉ 355 rue McGill ☎ 514/380-2222 or 866/380-2202 🚇 Square-Victoria

W MONTRÉAL

wmontrealhotel.com

Black, yellow, gold and white are the dominant colours at this chic, modern, design hotel situated in the historic Bank of Canada building on the border between downtown and Old Montréal.

➕ E12 ✉ 901 Square-Victoria ☎ 514/395-3100 or 888/627-7081 🚇 Square-Victoria

CHILDREN

Some hotels have family-plan deals that allow children sharing a room with their parents to stay (and sometimes eat) free. Most rooms have two double beds and some provide a third, smaller bed in the same room for a modest fee. More expensive hotels may offer child-minding services and children's programs. Swimming pools and electronic games and movies make some hotels particularly child-friendly.

Here is key information to help smooth your path before you go and when you arrive. Get savvy with the local transportation, explore the Montréal websites or check out what festivals are taking place.

Planning Ahead

When to Go

The best time to visit Montréal is between late May and late October. The summer, from the end of June to the first weekend in September, is rich in festivals. Fall brings cooler weather, better for walking; the parks can be spectacular. In winter, a visit can be coupled with a trip to a ski resort.

TIME

Montréal operates on Eastern Standard Time, 3 hours ahead of Los Angeles, 5 hours behind London.

AVERAGE DAILY MAXIMUM TEMPERATURES

JAN	FEB	MAR	APR	MAY	JUN	JUL	AUG	SEP	OCT	NOV	DEC
18°F	20°F	31°F	45°F	63°F	73°F	79°F	77°F	69°F	56°F	43°F	33°F
-8°C	-7°C	-1°C	7°C	17°C	23°C	26°C	25°C	21°C	13°C	6°C	1°C

Spring (April to May) The leap between winter and summer can be very abrupt. It is also the least attractive time of year as the melting snow reveals dead grass littered with the debris of winter.

Summer (June to August) begins on June 24, the date of the *Québec Fête National*. The city can be very hot and humid, especially in downtown.

Fall (September to October), with cooler temperatures and sunny days, makes for ideal exploring. There are fewer visitors, so you can see the city as the locals do.

Winter (November to March), Montréal's defining season, can be brutally cold, with occasional blizzards that shut down the city. There's often a brief thaw in January.

WHAT'S ON

January/February *Fête des Neiges*: Celebrations in Parc Jean-Drapeau.

February *Montréal High Lights Festival:* Celebrates winter with culinary and cultural events.

March *St. Patrick's Day Parade*.

May *Festival Trans-Ameriques*: New drama.

June *Grand Prix du Canada*: Formula 1 on Île Notre-Dame.

Tour d'Île: 40,000 bicyclists try this 50km (31-mile) trek through the city streets.

Suoni Per il Popolo: North America's largest avant-garde music festival.

Fringe Festival: Theater, dance and music.

June–July *Montréal International Jazz Festival*: The largest celebration of jazz music in the world brings top names in jazz to perform in concerts, many of them free.

International Fireworks Competition: Saturdays (mid-June to mid-July).

July *Juste Pour Rire (Just for Laughs)*: The world's largest comedy festival.

Nuits d'Afrique: Traditional African music and festivities on boulevard Saint-Laurent.

Franco Folies: 1,000 musicians take part in a celebration of French songs and music.

August *Divers/Cité*: Five days of gay pride events.

Italian Week: A week of Italian music, theater, food and other fun.

Festival des Films du Monde: World film festival.

October *Festival du Nouveau Cinéma*: Independent and avant-garde films/videos.

Montréal Online

mtlblog.com
A news and lifestyle blog that looks at all things Montréal.

montrealplus.ca
Information about Montréal lodging, dining, shopping and entertainment.

vieux.montreal.qc.ca
A comprehensive guide to historic Vieux-Montréal. Includes live webcams, maps and historical information and tours.

montrealgazette.com
News and features from the *Montréal Gazette,* the city's daily newspaper.

mtl.org
You can download maps, print itineraries and read up on attractions and coming events on this, the official tourist information website.

montrealjazzfest.com
A venue map, ticket information and performer news for Montréal's largest festival, the *Festival International de Jazz de Montréal.*

hahaha.com
The site has news of this year's festival and ticket information about the Just for Laughs comedy festival.

parcjeandrapeau.com
Information on tourist attractions and events in the Parc Jean-Drapeau; also maps and history.

restomontreal.ca
Narrow your search for the perfect meal by key-word or district on this funky restaurant site.

smartshoppingmontreal.com
Updated daily to bring the latest news on sales and special deals on everything from high fashion to a factory outlet for Kosher sweets.

TRAVEL SITES

fodors.com
A complete travel-planning site. You can research prices and weather; book air tickets, cars and rooms; ask questions (and get answers) from fellow travelers; and find links to other sites.

montreal.com
Exhaustive lists of what to do, and where to sleep and eat. You'll find information for all tastes, from tourist sights to local activities.

WIFI

Montréal's free Wifi network can be accessed all over the downtown core, including the Old Port and the Quartier des Spectacles. Most cafés, including ubiquitous fast-food chain Tim Horton's, also offer free Wifi.

FINDING TICKETS

La Vitrine at the place des Arts (2 rue Sainte-Catherine Ouest ☎ 514/285-4545; lavitrine.com) is the place to get tickets to all Montréal events, and the best place for last-minute tickets.

FLYING TIMES

Airport gate to airport gate, Montréal is about an hour by air from New York City; two hours from Chicago; four hours 30 minutes from Dallas; six hours from Los Angeles; six hours from London; and 22 hours from Sydney.

ARRIVING BY TAXI

Taxis charge a set fare of around $42 (plus tip) from the airport to central downtown locations, from the Vieux-Montréal district to near avenue Les Pins, between Atwater and Papineau.

AIRPORTS

Montréal-Trudeau Airport is 22.5km (14 miles) southwest of the city and handles all commercial flights. Aéroport de Mirabel is 56km (35 miles) northwest of the city and handles flights by private planes.

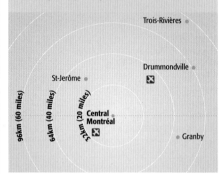

Trois-Rivières

Drummondville

St-Jerôme

96km (60 miles)

64km (40 miles)

32km (20 miles)

Central Montréal

Granby

ARRIVING BY AIR

Montréal's main airport for international and domestic flights is the Aéroport International Pierre-Elliott-Trudeau de Montréal (975 boulevard Roméo-Vachon Nord, Dorval; tel 514/ 394-7377; flight information toll-free in Canada 800/465-1213; admtl.com). The airport is more commonly known as Montréal-Trudeau or by its previous name, Dorval. Its international code is YUL. Considerable expansion and modernization have created a new international arrivals area and Transborder Zone for visitors to and from the United States. Passengers heading for the United States clear US Customs in Montréal before boarding, instead of at their US destination.

FROM THE AÉROPORT MONTRÉAL-TRUDEAU

If you are on a tight budget, then it is possible to use public transportation to reach the city, though it can be a slow process. Allow 60–90 minutes. Use the dedicated 747 bus line (tel 514/868-3737 or 514/786-4636; stm.info), which runs from the airport in front of the main terminal building to the main bus station (Station Centrale Berri, 505 boulevard de

Maisonneuve). En route it stops at or close to many of the city's main downtown hotels and attractions. Services depart regularly 24 hours a day, seven days a week (usually every 10 minutes, half-hourly and hourly through the night). Tickets can be obtained from the airport, bus-station ticket kiosks, Métro stations or the Hilton hotel downtown. The cost is $10, with reductions for senior citizens and children between 5 and 12. Children under 5 travel free. You will need the correct change to buy tickets on board the bus. The ticket is valid across the STM transit network for 24 hours.

Free minibus shuttles run from the bus station to around 40 downtown, Vieux-Montréal and Quartier-Latin hotels, but check to see if you wouldn't be better off disembarking from the 747 service earlier and walking directly to your hotel. Seats can be pre-booked by calling 514/631-1856.

ARRIVING BY TRAIN
Canadian trains run by VIA Rail (514/989-2626 or 888/842-7245 in Québec; viarail.ca) and US trains operated by Amtrak (800/872-7245; amtrak.com) all arrive at Montréal's main railway station, the Gare Centrale (Central Station), behind the Fairmont Le Reine Elizabeth hotel at 895 rue de la Gauchetière Ouest. The station is connected to the Underground City at several points, and to the Bonaventure Métro station.

ARRIVING BY BUS
Montréal's Station Centrale d'Autobus at 505 boulevard de Maisonneuve Est (514/842-2281; gamtl.com) has connections to the Berri-UQAM Métro station. It handles all Greyhound (greyhound.ca) and other long-distance bus services from Canadian and some US cities, including Orléans Express (orleansexpress.com), which covers most routes in Québec province. The quickest buses to Québec City and Ottawa take 2 hours 20 minutes. Buses from New York take 8 hours and 7 hours from Boston.

ARRIVING BY CAR
Montréal is 47km (29 miles) from the US border, and is accessed from New York City on the New York State Thruway (I-87), which in Canada becomes Route 15. Or you can take US I-89 north until it becomes Route 133 that then becomes Highway 35, from which you turn onto Route 10, a road that leads straight to Montréal's downtown. Coming from Massachusetts, follow I-91, and then pick up Route 55 and Route 10 through the Eastern Townships area to Montréal. From Boston, take I-93, I-89 and Route 133. If coming from elsewhere in Canada, use the Trans-Canada Highway (Highway 1), which crosses the city as Route 40, then Route 25, before heading eastward as Route 20. The main roads from Toronto and Ottawa are Routes 401 and 417 respectively. They converge west of Montréal, where you can pick up Routes 20 or 40.

Getting Around

TRAVEL INSURANCE

Travel insurance, including coverage for medical costs, is strongly recommended. Check your insurance coverage and buy a supplementary policy as needed.

VISITORS WITH DISABILITIES

Montréal's Métro system is not adapted for wheelchairs. There are few elevators and the escalators are not always dependable, so deep stations such as Snowdon and Lucien-L'Allier are difficult for anyone with mobility problems. The new, low-slung buses are a little better. Passengers with a cane or crutches can embark with care. They also accept wheelchairs at the rear exit doors, but space is limited and the entrance tight. Most major attractions and hotels are much better, with ramps and elevators, and facilities to help hearing- and vision-impaired visitors. For additional information contact Kéroul ✉ 4545 avenue Pierre-De-Coubertin, Box 1000, Branch M, Montréal, H1V 0B2 ☎ 514/252-3104; keroul.qc.ca.

Montréal has 192 bus routes and a Métro system with 68 stations and links to more than 32km (20 miles) of walkways in the Underground City (514/786-4636; stm.info).

● There are four color-coded lines (green, orange, blue and yellow).

● Buy flat-fare one-way tickets that are valid for 2 hours, either as singles ($3.25) or a discounted two-trip ticket ($3 per trip) at Métro booths and some retailers, but not on buses.

● Tickets are good on both the Métro and the buses (exclusions include the 747 airport service), but if you have to change from one to the other, get a transfer from your bus driver or from the machine in the Métro station where your journey started.

● Ten-trip tickets ($27), an unlimited weekend pass ($13.75), weekly ($25.75) and monthly ($83) passes are also available.

● Multi-day multi-ride Métro/bus passes are $18 for three days, $10 for one day.

● An unlimited travel evening ticket (6pm to 5am the next morning) is available for $5.

● Children under 5 years old are free, as are accompanied children aged 11 or under on weekends and some holidays.

● Bus passengers with no ticket or pass must have the exact fare.

● The orange and green lines operate Sunday to Friday 5.30am–12.30am, and Saturday 5.30am–1am.

● The blue line runs daily between 5.30am and 12.15am.

● The yellow line runs 5.30am–1am Monday to Friday and Sunday, and 5.30am–1.30am on Saturday.

● Most buses keep running until around 12.30am, when a night service takes over on limited routes.

ROUTES AND TICKETS

● See the STM (Société de Transport de Montréal) website stm.info or visit the Mezzanine Level, Berri-UQAM Métro Station (tel 514/786-4636); open Mon–Fri 8–6.

MÉTRO AND BUS SERVICES

● Four key stations provide the main interchanges between lines: Berri-UQAM (orange, green and yellow lines); Lionel-Groulx (green and orange); Snowdon (blue and orange); Jean-Talon (blue and orange).

● A one-day or three-day pass allows you to travel at will on buses or Métro. For further information call 514/786-4636. Both may be purchased from selected Métro stations, the tourist office or downtown hotels.

● Commuter trains are operated by AMT (Agence Métropolitaine de Transport) on five lines with 45 stations. They go to Dorion-Rigaud in the west, Deux-Montagnes and Blainville-Saint-Jérôme, both to the north, Mont-Saint-Hilaire, across the river to the east, and Delson-Candiac, south across the river. These services are limited to immediately before and after normal business hours. For more information visit amt.qc.ca.

TAXIS

Taxis stand outside main hotels, near the train station and at major intersections, and can be hailed on the street. Cab companies include:

● Co-op (tel 514/636-6666), cooptaxi.com
● Diamond (tel 514/273-6331), taxidiamond.com
● A 10–15 percent tip is normal.

CAR RENTAL

To rent a car in Montréal you must be 25 or over (21 if using a major credit card).

● Avis 1225 rue Metcalfe (tel 514/866-2847 or 800/879-2847)
● Budget 895 rue de la Gauchetière (tel 514/866-7675)
● Hertz Canada 1073 rue Drummond (tel 514/938-1717 or 800/654-3131 (English), 800/263-0678 (French)
● Thrifty-Québec 159 rue Saint-Antoine Ouest (tel 514/875-1100)
● National 1200 rue Stanley (tel 514/878-2771 or 800/227-7368)

WATERWAY TRANSPORT

It's worth taking a boat just to see some of the city from the river. Navettes Maritimes du St-Laurent (☎ 514/281-8000 or 866/228-3280; navettesmaritimes.com) runs ferries from Jacques Cartier Pier in the Vieux-Port to the Réal Bouvier Marina in Longueuil.
Boats leave hourly from Montréal: mid-May to mid-Jun and early Sep to early Oct Sat, Sun 9.35–6.35; mid-Jun to early Sep Mon–Thu 9.35–6.35, Sat–Sun 8.35–10.35. From Longueuil start and finish times are a half-hour later.

TOURIST OFFICE

Montréal's main tourist office is the **Centre Infotouriste** bonjourquebec.com
✉ 1255 rue Peel, Bureau 100 ☎ 514/873-2015 or 877/266-5687 in Canada and the US 🕐 Jun–Labor Day daily 7am–8pm; Labor Day–May daily 9–6
🚇 Peel

Essential Facts

ENTRY REQUIREMENTS

Citizens of EU and most British Commonwealth countries require a valid passport and a return or onward ticket. US citizens returning from abroad (including Canada) by land, sea or air need to show a valid passport or other documents. People under 18 must have a parent or guardian letter stating a length of stay. If children are traveling with a divorced parent who shares custody, that parent must carry the legal custody documents. If children are traveling with adults who are not parents or guardians, those adults must carry the written permission of the parents or guardians.

Visitors from certain countries who are flying into Canada (but not entering by land or sea) need to obtain an Electronic Travel Authorization, to be presented with their passport at check-in. This includes British citizens and legal permanent residents of the US; the latter also need to show their Green Card. For a list of the countries concerned, visit: cic.gc.ca/english/visit/visas-all.asp For visa requirements, visit: cic.gc.ca/english/visit/apply-who.asp.

ELECTRICITY

● Current in Canada is 110 volts AC (60Hz). Plug adaptors are needed to match the two-prong sockets.

MAIL

● You can find the location of main and smaller post offices at canadapost.ca
● Smaller post offices are inside shops, department stores and train stations wherever there are Postes Canada signs.
● Buy stamps from post offices, the Centre Infotouriste in rue Peel, train stations and bus terminals, the airport and stores.
● Within Canada, postcards and letters up to 30g are 63¢; 30–50g $1.10; over 50g $1.34. Cards and letters to the US cost $1.10 up to 30g. Rates for other destinations are $1.85 up to 30g and $2.68 from 30 to 50g.
● Letters sent for collection in hotels should be marked "Guest Mail, Hold for Arrival."

MONEY

Canadian dollars are the local currency, although US dollars and ATM cards are widely accepted. French speakers often call a penny a "sou," the nickel "cinq sous" and the quarter "vingt-cinq sous." English speakers call the dollar coin a "looney" after the bird (a loon) on its obverse and the bimetal $2 coin a "tooney."

OPENING HOURS

● Shops: hours vary but are typically Mon–Fri 9 or 9.30–6, Sat 9–5. Some open Sun 12–5. Some stores open Thu, Fri 10–9, Sat 10–6, Sun 12–5.
● Banks: Mon–Fri 9–4. Some larger banks open Sat morning.
● Post offices: Mon–Fri 8.30–5.30. Some open Sat mornings.
● Restaurants: hours vary, but many of the city's eating places may only open for lunch Mon–Fri and only offer dinner on Sat, or on limited other evenings during the week, usually from Thu. Some restaurants may close Sun and Mon.

PUBLIC HOLIDAYS
● January 1; Good Friday; Easter Monday; Victoria Day (3rd Mon in May); *Fête Nationale* (June 24); Canada Day (July 1); Labor Day (1st Mon in Sep); Thanksgiving (second Mon in Oct); December 25. Remembrance Day (Nov 11) is also widely observed.

SALES TAX
● Taxes are generally added to the displayed prices of goods in the stores, hotel rates, restaurant checks, car rental, etc, so you need to do a bit of mental arithmetic before deciding whether or not you have found a bargain. When tipping in a restaurant, you calculate the amount on the pre-tax total.
● There are two levels of sales tax: the federal Goods and Services Tax (GST), which is currently 5 percent; and the Québec provincial tax (TVQ or QST) of 9.975 percent. Hotel guests are also charged 3 percent tax per night.
● Tax refunds are no longer offered to visitors to Canada.

TELEPHONES
● Phone booths are very very rare these days.
● Information for local numbers can be reached by dialing 411 or online at 411.ca.
● For a number outside the area you are in, dial 1, then the area code.
● Direct dial phones are common in many hotels and motels. A surcharge is levied, but some offer free local calls.
● Many organizations have toll-free numbers—800, 866, 888 or 877 prefix. Some operate within a province, others in Canada, and a few across North America. Dial 1 first.
● To call the US from Canada dial the area code and the number. To call the UK from Canada dial 011 44, followed by the area code (minus its first zero), and the number required.
● To call Canada from the US dial 1, the area code, and then the number. To call Canada from the UK dial 001, then the area code, and then the number.

USEFUL NUMBERS
American Express ☎ 800/869-3016; americanexpress.com
MasterCard ☎ 800/307-7309; mastercard.com
Visa ☎ 800/847-2911; visa.com
Road breakdown ☎ 800/222-4357 or 514/861-1313

EMERGENCY NUMBERS
Police, fire, ambulance ☎ 911 or dial 0.
Lost and found Bus or Métro ✉ Mezzanine Level, Berri-UQAM Métro ☎ 514/786-4636 🕐 Mon–Fri 8–6. Elsewhere contact the MUC Police (spvm.wc.ca)
US Consulate ✉ 1155 rue Saint-Alexandre ☎ 514/398-9695, montreal.usconsulate.gov
US Embassy ✉ 490 Sussex Drive, Ottawa ☎ 613/688-5335; canada.usembassy.gov
UK Consulate ✉ 2000 McGill College Avenue, Suite 1940, Montréal ☎ 514/866-5863
British High Commission ✉ 80 Elgin Street, Ottawa ☎ 613/237-1530; gov.uk
Irish Embassy ✉ 130 Albert Street, Suite 1105, 11th Floor, Ottawa ☎ 613/233-6281; embassyofireland.ca

Language

BASIC VOCABULARY

oui/non	yes/no
s'il vous plaît	please
merci	thank you
excusez-moi	excuse me
bonjour	hello
bonsoir	good evening
au revoir	goodbye
parlez-vous anglais?	do you speak English?
je ne comprends pas	I don't understand
combien?	how much?
où est/sont…?	where is/are…?
ici/là	here/there
tournez à gauche/droite	turn left/right
tout droit	straight on
quand?	when?
aujourd'hui	today
hier	yesterday
demain	tomorrow
combien de temps?	how long?
à quelle heure?	at what time?
à quelle heure ouvrez/ fermez-vous?	what time do you open/ close?
avez-vous…?	do you have…?
une chambre simple	a single room
une chambre double	a double room
avec/sans salle de bains	with/without bathroom
le petit déjeuner	breakfast
le déjeuner	lunch
le dîner	dinner
c'est combien?	how much is this?
acceptez-vous des cartes de credit?	do you take credit cards?
j'ai besoin d'un médecin/dentiste	I need a doctor/ dentist
pouvez-vous m'aider?	can you help me?
où est l'hôpital?	where is the hospital?
où est le commissariat?	where is the police station?

NUMBERS

un	1
deux	2
trois	3
quatre	4
cinq	5
six	6
sept	7
huit	8
neuf	9
dix	10
onze	11
douze	12
treize	13
quatorze	14
quinze	15
seize	16
dix-sept	17
dix-huit	18
dix-neuf	19
vingt	20
vingt-et-un	21
trente	30
quarante	40
cinquante	50
soixante	60
soixante-dix	70
quatre-vingts	80
quatre-vingt- dix	90
cent	100
mille	1,000

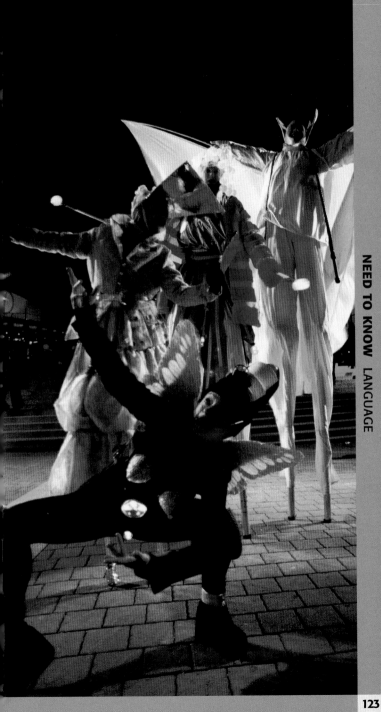

Timeline

EARLY DAYS

In 1535 French explorer Jacques Cartier became the first European to set foot in the native village of Hochelaga, site of modern-day Montréal. He named the hill above the village Mont-Royal—this was translated to Mont-Real by Italian writer G. B. Ramuso in 1556.

BANK RAID

Montréal was the staging ground of the only Confederate raid on New England during the Civil War in the United States. On October 19, 1864, 20 cavalrymen swooped down on St. Albans, Vermont. The raiders robbed three banks and made off with more than $200,000 before the stunned Vermonters could react. The raiders were arrested in Montréal.

1642 Paul de Chomedey, a French soldier, establishes Ville-Marie on the island of Montréal. He is helped by Jeanne Mance.

1663 King Louis XIV of France gives land rights on Île de Mont-Real to the Sulpicians, a proselytising religious order.

1682 Ville-Marie becomes HQ of the Compagnie du Nordouest, fur-trading rivals of the Hudson's Bay Company.

1701 The French sign a treaty with the native Iroquois, ending more than 50 years of conflict following the Iroquois massacre of the Hurons, allies of the French, in 1649.

1710 The name Ville-Marie is dropped.

1754–63 The French and Indian War breaks out between England and France. In 1759 General James Wolfe is mortally wounded during the capture of French Québec and in 1760 the British take Montréal. The 1763 Treaty of Paris cedes Canada to Britain.

1775 American revolutionary troops occupy Montréal in an effort to enlist French Canadians to their cause.

1832 Montréal is North America's second-largest city.

1844 Montréal becomes the capital of the new United Province of Canada.

1867 The Dominion of Canada is formed: Québec, Ontario, New Brunswick, Nova Scotia.

1940 Colorful mayor Camillien Houde is interned after urging Canadians not to register for wartime conscription.

1959 The Saint Lawrence Seaway opens.

1969 Canada's federal government accepts both French and English as official languages.

1970 Nationalist terrorists kidnap a provincial cabinet minister and a British diplomat, triggering one of Canada's worst political crises. The Québec government makes French the province's only official language.

1995 50 percent of Québécois vote to remain part of Canada, but in Montréal almost 70 percent vote against independence.

2009 Montréal creates a 1km sq block—the Quartier des Spectacles—devoted entirely to culture, entertainment and festivals.

2014 Separatist Parti Québécois is heavily defeated in Québec's general election after only one term in office.

2017 Montréal celebrates the 375th anniversary of its founding.

2017 Valérie Plante becomes first woman to be elected mayor (*mairesse*) of Montréal.

ACHIEVEMENTS

● The opening of the Lachine Canal in 1825 allows ships to travel between the Atlantic and the Great Lakes.

● The completion of the Canadian Pacific Railway in 1886 links Montréal to the Pacific coast, helping the city to develop into the financial and industrial capital of Canada.

● Montréal's Expo '67 world fair, celebrating Canada's centennial, attracts 53 million visitors.

● Montréal hosts the summer Olympic Games in 1976.

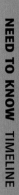

A view of early Montréal and fortifications (far left); a portrait of Major General James Wolfe (middle left); a picture depicts the death of General Wolfe (middle right); Montréal in winter, an ice jam (right)

Index

Montréal 25 Best

WRITTEN BY Tim Jepson
UPDATED BY Elizabeth Warkentin
SERIES EDITOR Clare Ashton
COVER DESIGN Chie Ushio, Yuko Inagaki
DESIGN WORK Tom Whitlock and Liz Baldin
IMAGE RETOUCHING AND REPRO Ian Little

Published in the United Kingdom by AA Publishing

ISBN 978-1-64097-093-9

NINTH EDITION

Color separation by AA Digital Department
Printed and bound by Leo Paper Products, China

10 9 8 7 6 5 4 3 2 1

A05593
Maps in this title produced from mapping © MAIRDUMONT / Falk Verlag 2013
Data from openstreetmap.org © Open Street Map contributors
Transport map © Communicarta Ltd, UK

The Automobile Association would like to thank the following photographers, companies and picture libraries for their assistance in the preparation of this book.

2/3t Courtesy of Tourisme Montréal; **4/5t** Courtesy of Tourisme Montréal; **4tl** AA/C Coe; **5b** AA/J F Pin; **6/7t** Courtesy of Tourisme Montréal; **6cl** Pierre Girard; **6c** AA/J F Pin; **6cr** AA/J F Pin; **6bl** AA/J F Pin; **6bc** AA/J F Pin; **6br** Courtesy of Canadian Tourism Commission; **7cl** Courtesy of Tourisme Montréal; **7c** AA/J F Pin; **7cr** AA/N Sumner; **7bl** Courtesy of Biodôme de Montréal; **7bc** AA/J F Pin; **7br** Courtesy of Les Ballets Jazz de Montréal; **8/9t** Courtesy of Tourisme Montréal; **10/11t** Courtesy of Tourisme Montréal; **10tr** Courtesy of Tourisme Montréal, Stephan Poulin; **10bcr** Mark Tomalty; **10br** AA/M Dent; **11tl** Courtesy of Tourisme Montréal, Stephan Poulin; **11cl** Courtesy of Tourisme Quebec, Linda Turgeon; **11bl** AA/C Coe; **12/3t** Courtesy of Tourisme Montréal; **13tl** Courtesy of Tourisme Montréal, Stephan Poulin; **13tcl** Courtesy of Casino de Montréal; **13cl** AA/J F Pin; **13bcl** Courtesy of Les Ballets Jazz de Montréal; **13b** Courtesy of Canadian Tourism Commission; **14/15t** Courtesy of Tourisme Montréal; **14tr** AA/P Kenward; **14tcr** Courtesy of Tourisme Montréal, Stephan Poulin; **14bcr** Courtesy of Tourisme Montréal, Stephan Poulin; **14br** Courtesy of Tourisme Montréal, Stephan Poulin; **16/17t** Courtesy of Tourisme Montréal; **16/7b** Lionela Rob/Alamy; **16ct** Courtesy of Tourisme Montréal, Stephan Poulin; **16c** AA/J F Pin; **16cb** Courtesy of Tourisme Montréal, Stephan Poulin; **17ct** Courtesy of Tourisme Montréal, Stephan Poulin; **17c** Courtesy of Canadian Tourism Commission; **17cb** Pierre Rochon/Alamy; **18t** Courtesy of Tourisme Montréal; **18tr** Courtesy of Tourisme Montréal, Stephan Poulin; **18bcr** Courtesy of Tourisme Montréal, Stephan Poulin; **18br** AA/J F Pin; **19t** Courtesy of Tourisme Montréal, Stephan Poulin; **19tc** AA/J F Pin; **19c** Courtesy of Tourisme Montréal; **19bc** AA/J F Pin; **19b** Courtesy of Parc Jean-Drapeau; **20/1** Courtesy of Tourisme Montréal, Stephan Poulin; **24l** Courtesy of Canadian Tourism Commission; **24/5** AA/J F Pin; 26tl AA/J F Pin; **26tc** AA/J F Pin; **26tr** AA/J F Pin; **27tl** AA/M Bonnet; **27tr** AA/M Bonnet; **28/29** AA/M Bonnet; **30l** AA/M Bonnet; **30r** AA/M Bonnet; **31** Marc Bruxelle/Alamy Stock Photo; **32** All Canada Photos/Alamy; **33t** AA/J F Pin; **33bl** AA/J F Pin; **33br** AA/M Bonnet; **34t** AA/J F Pin; **34b** AA/M Bonnet; **35t** AA/J F Pin; **35bl** AA/M Bonnet; **36/7t** AA/J F Pin; **36bl** AA/M Bonnet; **36br** Bill Brooks/Alamy ; **37bl** AA/J F Pin; **37br** Maria Janicki/Alamy Stock Photo; **38t** AA/J F Pin; **38bl** Paul Carstairs/Alamy; **38br** Maria Janicki/Alamy Stock Photo; **39t** AA/J F Pin; **40t** Courtesy of Tourisme Montréal, Stephan Poulin; **41t** AA/M Chaplow; **42t** Courtesy of Tourisme Montréal, Stephan Poulin; **43t** AA/C Sawyer; **44t** AA/C Sawyer; **45** AA/J F Pin; **48tl** AA/J F Pin; **48tr** AA/J F Pin; **49tl** Courtesy of Canadian Centre for Architecture; **49tc** Courtesy of Canadian Centre for Architecture; **49tr** Courtesy of Canadian Centre for Architecture; **50tl** AA/M Bonnet; **50tr** AA/M Bonnet; 51tl AA/M Bonnet; **51tr** AA/M Bonnet; **52l** AA/M Bonnet; **52/53t** AA/M Bonnet; **52/53c** AA/M Bonnet; **53tl** AA/M Bonnet; **53r** AA/M Bonnet; **54l** AA/J F Pin; **54r** AA/J F Pin; **55tl** AA/M Bonnet; **55tc** AA/M Bonnet; **55tr** AA/M Bonnet; **56tl** AA/M Bonnet; **56tc** AA/M Bonnet; **56tr** AA/M Bonnet; **57tl** AA/M Bonnet; **57tc** AA/M Bonnet; **57tr** AA/M Bonnet; **58/9t** AA/J F Pin; **58b** Courtesy of Tourisme Montréal, Stephan Poulin; **59bl** AA/M Bonnet; **59br** AA/M Bonnet; **60** AA/J F Pin; **61** Courtesy of Tourisme Montréal, Stephan Poulin; **62t** Courtesy of Tourisme Montréal, Stephan Poulin; **63t** Photodisc; **64t** AA/J F Pin; **65t** Montréal Crudessence/ Michael Julian Berz; **66t** Montréal Crudessence/Michael Julian Berz; **67** Courtesy of Tourisme Montréal, Stephan Poulin; **70/71** AA/M Bonnet; **71t** AA/M Bonnet; **71cl** AA/M Bonnet; **71cr** AA/M Bonnet; **72/73** AA/M Bonnet; **73t** AA/M Bonnet; **73cl** AA/M Bonnet; **73cr** AA/M Bonnet; **74l** Megapress/Alamy; **74r** AA/S McBride; **75t** AA/J F Pin; **75b** AA/M Bonnet; **76t** AA/J F Pin; **76b** AA/M Bonnet; **77t** AA/J F Pin; **78t** Courtesy of Tourisme Montréal, Stephan Poulin; **79** Tibor Bognor/Alamy Stock Photo; **80t** Digitalvision; **81t** Courtesy of Tourisme Quebec, Linda Turgeon; **82t** AA/C Sawyer; **83** Courtesy of Biodôme de Montréal; **86tl** AA/M Bonnet; **86bl** AA/M Bonnet; **86br** AA/M Bonnet; **86/87tc** AA/M Bonnet; **86/87bc** AA/M Bonnet; **87bl** AA/M Bonnet; **87r** AA/J F Pin; **88l** AA/M Bonnet; **88/89t** AA/M Bonnet; **88/89c** AA/M Bonnet; **89t** AA/M Bonnet; **89c** AA/M Bonnet; **90** Courtesy of Regie des Installations Olympiques; **91l** AA/M Bonnet; **91r** AA/M Bonnet; **92t** AA/J F Pin; **92b** Gilles Rivest; **93t** AA/J F Pin; **93b** AA/M Bonnet; **94t** Courtesy of Canadian Tourism Commission; **94c** AA/M Bonnet; **95** AA/J F Pin; **98l** Megapress/Alamy; **98/99t** AA/C Sawyer; **98/99b** Paul-Émile Cadorette; **99t** Jeff Greenberg/Alamy; **99b** AA/C Sawyer; **100c** NielsVK/Alamy; **101l** Courtesy of Tourisme Montréal, Stephan Poulin; **101tr** Courtesy of Tourisme Montréal, Stephan Poulin; **101br** cunningeye/Alamy; **102t** Courtesy of Grand Prix F1 of Canada; **102bl** AA/M Bonnet; **102br** AA/M Bonnet; **103t** AA/M Bonnet; **103cl** AA/M Bonnet; **103cr** AA/M Bonnet; **104t** AA/J F Pin; **104b** AA/M Bonnet; **105t** AA/J F Pin; **105b** AA/M Bonnet; **106** AA/M Bonnet; **107** AA/M Bonnet; **108/109t** AA/C Sawyer; **18tcl** Courtesy of Inter-Continental Montréal; **108c** Courtesy of Hotel St-Paul; **108bcr** Courtesy of Hotel St.-Paul; **108br** Courtesy of Tourisme Montréal, Stephan Poulin; **110/111t** AA/C Sawyer; **112t** AA/C Sawyer; **113** Courtesy of Tourisme Montréal, Stephan Poulin; **114/115t** AA/J F Pin; **116/117t** AA/J F Pin; **118/119t** AA/J F Pin; **120/121t** AA/J F Pin; **122t** AA/J F Pin; **123** Courtesy of Tourisme Montréal, Stephan Poulin; **124/125t** AA/J F Pin; **124bl** AA; **124br** AA; **124/125bc** AA; **125br** AA

Every effort has been made to trace the copyright holders, and we apologise in advance for any accidental errors. We would be happy to apply the corrections in the following edition of this publication.

Titles in the Series